Power of Human Resources

Power of Human Resources

Fawziya Al Araimi

authorHOUSE®

AuthorHouse™
1663 Liberty Drive
Bloomington, IN 47403
www.authorhouse.com
Phone: 1-800-839-8640

First published by AuthorHouse   08/11/2011

ISBN: 978-1-4567-8671-7 (sc)
ISBN: 978-1-4567-8670-0 (hc)
ISBN: 978-1-4567-8669-4 (ebk)

Printed in the United States of America

Dedication

H.M. Sultan Qaboos bin Said

A Special Dedication

I would like to specially dedicate this book as my personal humble tribute to H.M. Sultan Qaboos bin Said, the Sultan of Oman. As the most benevolent ruler of our proud nation, H.M. Sultan Qaboos has remarkably transformed Oman into one of the most prosperous nations of the Gulf and the Middle East Region. As the father of modern Oman, H.M. Sultan Qaboos has been the principal architect to have ushered in the new dawn of Omani Renaissance that has brought great wealth, prosperity and happiness for every Omani citizen. We are indeed, one and all; grateful to H.M. Sultan Qaboos for providing us with his exemplary leadership and pragmatic vision that has shaped the very anvil for carving the modern destiny of our nation. As Omanis, we all feel fortunate and blessed to have been provided with the challenge and the opportunity to participate and contribute to the ongoing renaissance for further improving and developing our great nation. H.M. Sultan Qaboos has reiterated on many occasions that providing adequate attention to the development of human resources, helping in unleashing of the creative talents within people and equipping people with the technological knowhow for improving human performance holds the key for genuine national development and progress. In the Sultan's own words "it must be remembered that since the human element is the maker of the renaissance and the builder of a civilization, no effort must be spared in honing, developing and training our human resources".

My writing of this book on HR and its infinite potential is thus largely based on the inspiration that I have drawn from His Majesty the Sultan of Oman's charismatic leadership, motivational words of wisdom and his relentless support for the development of our national human resources. I sincerely hope that this book would succeed in making its humble contribution towards greater realization of the centrality of human resources for modern firms and the multidimensional benefits that HR can offer for the enlightened management of public and private sector entities.

Fawziya Bint Ghazi Bin Juma Al Araimi

CONTENTS

PREFACE

The face of modern HR has been quite remarkably transformed. HR today has emerged as a strategic partner, an employee champion, and a change agent for modern organizations. Attracting, recruiting and retaining employees has become a quintessential necessity for gaining competitive edge, improving profitability, inspiring and sustaining employee motivation. Gone are the days when HR was considered a peripheral entity and often had to face the gauntlet during times of recession, today HR is not just needed for improving overall organizational performance but is considered an integral and crucial part and parcel of any type of organization. HR plays a key role in defining not just parameters of success for modern firms but the very foundations of their existence. The present business landscape that companies operate in strongly underlines the importance, role and benefits that HR frameworks can bring forth for any modern organization. Human Resource Management is a multidimensional paradigm that showers myriad benefits for one and all; be it the investors, the management, the employees or even the customers.

Given the increased centrality and importance of HR, a need has always been felt that there must be a comprehensive yet practical and easy to read book on HR. While there has been a proliferation of many books on HR, most of them lack a comprehensive focus on dealing with an all encompassing paradigm such as HR and fail to make the right connections between HR and the overall organization. Books available in the market either tend to be too descriptive and conceptually oriented or tend to have an overt prescriptive focus. Books either tend to delve only into a few topics related to HR or just glance over the core topics of HRM in a superficial manner. This book thus aims to bridge the gaps in HR literature by creating a "one stop desk guide" that not only looks into relevant conceptual frameworks associated with HR but also outlines practical prescriptive frameworks that can prove useful for students, managers and even HR professionals.

This book covers all the core functions related to HR such as recruitment & selection, training & development, performance appraisal, compensation and job design. In addition the book also delves into new highly relevant areas such as (SHRM) Strategic human resource management, emotional intelligence and HR's role in management of change. Every chapter has been conveniently broken down into subtopics and finishes with a brief summary of useful take away points. The intent of the author is to cater to the needs of managers working in not just large companies but also in small and mid-sized companies who might be unfamiliar with the multifaceted domains or myriad benefits that are associated with the paradigm of human resources.

As an HR professional with more than two decades of HR management experience, it was my strong desire to write a book on HR that can be equally relevant for both the western world as well as Middle East and Arab nations. This book by amalgamating relevant conceptual, prescriptive and practical frameworks is the product of such an endeavour. I have always believed in the practical benefits and advantages that HR can bring forth for any company in improving its competitive edge, improving the workforce morale and in boosting overall organizational performance. We can no longer look at HR as an isolated or peripheral function but need to visualize it as a highly relevant and integral function for the whole organization. In the constantly evolving business landscape of modern times, it is imperative for the HR professionals to design, develop, demonstrate and deliver results through selection of appropriate HR practices that are in sync with the overall organizational mission, vision and objectives.

Modern HR professionals must not forget their overarching role and responsibility is not just towards the company but towards all the multiple stakeholders of an organization; be they investors, managers, employees or even customers.

Fawziya Bint Ghazi Bin Juma Al Araimi

CHAPTER 1

WHAT IS HR?

"If an organization is like a boat, then HR is its sail, you are sure to reach your destination if you know how to effectively steer the sail"

Fawziya Al Araimi

Effective People Management has emerged as the strategic new mantra for all modern corporations of the 21st century. Companies have progressively realized that their employees cannot be treated as peripheral entities rather need to be looked at as integral part and parcel of their organizations. Attracting, retaining and motivating employees has become the quintessential necessity for modern companies. After all it needs to be mentioned that organizations do not own people, but people run organizations. Therefore effective management of human resources not only ensures the very viability of the firms but also determines their profitability.

The face of modern HR seems to have changed dramatically over the years. HR can no longer be seen as a generic framework of administrative functions or processes for personnel management but rather has to be seen as a strategic business partner, a vital employee champion and a crucial change agent for the modern day companies.

The challenge of defining HR

To begin with, it would be interesting to find an answer to the multimillion dollar question regarding the definition of HR that seems to have plagued both the specialists and general practitioners. How do you define HR? What is HR? The answer to this question is not as simple and straightforward as it may seem. It can be pleasantly argued that there are as many definitions of HR as there are HR practitioners. For some HR can be defined as a sum total of generic processes that revolve around administrative functions concerning personnel management. For others, HR can be seen as a distinctive approach to employment management that focuses on gaining competitive advantage though the deployment of highly committed workforce.

I believe that HR can be generically defined as a range of activities under the rubric of employment relationship that are directed for attracting, retaining, developing and motivating employees. In other words HR should be seen as a set of distinct, interrelated activities, or processes that can help in developing the human capital pool, engender motivation and facilitate employee empowerment.

HR—A source of distinctive capabilities

Kay (1993) in his seminal work on foundations of corporate success states that there are three distinctive capabilities that help the modern firm create unique value and gain the much needed competitive edge. These distinctive capabilities are firm's architecture, firm's reputation and innovation (Kay, 1993). Architecture can be seen as the network of relational contracts within or around the firm in relation to its employees, customers and suppliers. Reputation can be seen as an important commercial mechanism for conveying information to consumers that can be developed based on product characteristics, quality and gradient of service offered. Innovation can add unique value by improving differentiation in product and service offerings. These three distinctive capabilities help the firm improve its uniqueness in relation to its competitors and provide it with its competitive edge.

While I agree with Kay (1993) in his outlining of distinctive capabilities, I strongly believe that all these capabilities are inherently dependent on the level and quality of HRM practices instituted within a firm. As far as a firm's architecture or its relationship contracts with its employees is concerned, it is quite natural to assume that HR department should assume the lead. Moreover such relational contracts with employees are not created in a vacuum but rather have to take into account the specificities of organizational relationship with reference to its suppliers and customers. A firm's reputation would also largely depend on how well the firm utilizes its human resource capabilities and the manner in which its employees can gel together to create uniqueness in the product offerings or quality of service provided. In a similar vein, innovation can be seen as a product of firm's human capital pool or the knowledge, skills and abilities that a company's work force has. So coming to think of it, every distinctive capability can be seen as inherently dependent on a firm's ability of utilizing productively the power of its human resources.

Linking HR to Performance—Fact or Fiction

Skeptics have often challenged the validity of the influence of HRM practices on organizational performance. Even some HR practitioners feel that the linkage between HR practices and firm's performance can be likened to a black box, which does not show clearly how HR can improve performance (Watson, 2004). I feel that the main problem with these skeptics is that they tend to overlook the fact that HR should be seen as an integrated and composite function, rather than seeing it as a detached or isolated component of the organization. Adoption of such a narrow "blinkers on approach" for viewing

3

HR prevents them from appreciating the multidimensional role and impact that HR can have for the organization. One cannot just look at isolated components of HR and then try to link each of these with organizational performance in terms of specific effects or influences. In doing so, what I feel the critics often overlook is the way in which different HRM practices create synergy and complementarities between and amongst themselves. If one were to tweak one aspect of HR then it should be natural to assume that a domino effect might be generated not only amongst different aspects of human resource management functions but also amongst the different aspects of a firm's operational and performance frameworks.

Critics often tend to ignore the fact that management of human resources is a social science, therefore unlike physical sciences, for every organizational facet 2 +2 does not always tantamount to 4. In fact, on account of different level of synergies and positive domino effects created by HRM practices, the sum total effect can be far more than the sum of the individual parts (Baron & Kreps, 1999). In the words of Aristotle, the overall impact of effective HR practices can lead to the "whole being far greater" than the sum of its individual parts.

HR : A victim of debates and controversies

It may be noted that the field of human resource management has been ravaged by a number of acrimonious debates regarding the very nature, content and focus of HR practices (Storey, 2001). From one perspective it is argued that companies should adopt a "hard HRM" focus wherein employees can be seen as yet another source for being exploited, on the other hand it is argued that the focus should be on development of "Soft HRM" practices that recognize the centrality of employees and is woven around the concept of commitment and mutuality. Similarly some proponents argue that modern firms would do well by adopting "high commitment" HR practices wherein the employers focus on developing a close psychological and emotional relationship with their employees by providing them with career and personal development opportunities. Others however want even the modern firms to focus on development of "low commitment" HRM practices wherein employer employee relationship is of the arms length type and workers are closely supervised and monitored. Some argue that HR is a reflection of objective reality; others go as far as calling it an empty game of rhetoric.

Regarding the aforementioned debates, as an HR practitioner with more than 2 decades of experience, I would like to forcefully emphasize that management of human resources should be seen as an art form. If HR management is an art form then is it wise to segregate HR into controversial fields of black or white? As HR practitioners the emphasis should be on developing flexibility in our understanding and openness in our vision to appreciate HR as an amalgamation of different shades of grey that can be created depending on the needs and requirements of the organization. One cannot and should not try to straight jacket a multidimensional framework such as HR into one specific slot or the other. HR cannot be thought of as only "soft or hard" because what appears to be soft on the outside may actually be masquerading the hard intentions of the company for improving the bottom line (Peters & Waterman, 1982). Similarly one cannot visualize HR practices as only oscillating between the two extremes of high commitment and low commitment practices, as every organization is different and the need for utilization of work force has to be seen in context of specifics of the organization, its competition and the general dynamics of the business landscape. The simplistic prescription of "one size fits all" approach just cannot work in context of a dynamic entity such as HR.

HR : Understanding the bigger picture

From my perspective, I visualize HR frameworks as a 360 degrees lens for the organization that facilitates in analyzing how different aspects of HRM relate to the organization as a whole as well as how different facets of the organization relate back to the HR frameworks. While HR symbolically can be regarded as a vital piece of the overall jigsaw puzzle of the organization, nevertheless unless and until we have idea about the broader canvass of the organization, one cannot understand how and where the different pieces of the puzzle would fit in. It is vital for all HR practitioners therefore to be well versed in not only the language of human resource management but also in the language of different departments of the organization such as business processes, marketing, finance and sales and how these connect or relate to HR. Given the multidimensional nature and focus of HRM, I believe that the field of human resource management cannot be seen as only the hallowed fiefdom of HR practitioners but rather needs to be seen as a flexible framework whose ownership has to be developed and shared by adopting a collaborative approach with all departments of an organization.

The face of modern HR has therefore been quite radically transformed. It cannot be seen as a relegated peripheral entity of personnel management but has to seen as a strategic business partner of the organization, an employee champion for improving employee participation and a change mentor that can help the organization deal positively with the winds of change. The need of the hour for effective management of human resources is therefore not for the development of micro specialists but in creation of macro generalists who understand the language of the whole organization and how the language of HR correlates with the language of other processes, functions and departments. HR professionals have to act as coaches, mentors and counselors for the employees in developing the unique human capital pool of the organization and through positive bundling of HR practices guide employees to elicit desired behavior, improve their levels of motivation, commitment, participation and empowerment.

HR : Adoption of a Balanced Score Card Approach

It seems clear that due to the multidimensional nature of HR, the increasing domain of influence of HRM, and the increasing perception of centrality of employees, adoption of balanced score card approach for dealing with Human Resource Management issues seems to be the right step for modern firms. Doing so, I believe allows the HR practitioners to receive a more holistic view of the entire organization and assess performance of HR from divergent perspectives. I would like to point out that Balanced score card method should not be considered as a new tool as it has served even earlier as a key strategic framework that helps in indexing performance related to different segments and areas of the organization.

Balanced score card method can help to align business activities of the organization with intended mission, vision and objectives of the organization, promote better areas for internal and external communication and monitor performance against well defined strategic goals (Kaplan & Norton, 1992). Application of Balanced Score card method to HRM does increase the responsibility of HR professionals for multiple stakeholders of the organization such as employees, customers and investors. The four domains associated with balanced score card are financial, customer, internal business processes, and learning and growth perspectives.

While HR does assume the leadership position in context of facilitating learning and growth perspective of employees for engendering their motivation, HR practitioners also have to be responsible for demonstrating how functions and processes of HR can relate to the satisfaction of consumer needs and improvement of business processes. The ultimate responsibility for HR professionals is to demonstrate how effective HRM practices can improve the financial or bottom line perspective of the organization. After all we are all here in business to make profits and what good is HR if it fails to deliver the intended financial results.

The new role framework for HR professionals: The crucial 4 Ds

Given that HR is such an all encompassing paradigm, I have always been confronted by questions from senior management that if HR managers are more than just people managers and can be seen as strategic business partners, coaches, and change agents, then is there any prescriptive role framework for modern age HR professionals? Is there any magical formula that can fulfill all the myriad expectations that a company has from its HR professionals?

From my perspective, I would like to provide a relatively simple and straightforward answer for all the above challenging questions. I feel that the new kind of role framework expected of HR professionals in modern times can be well represented by the 4D's Role framework—whereby HR professionals need to look at themselves as Designers, Developers, Demonstrators and Deliverers of competencies for the entire organization. Let me elaborate a bit further on my 4 D's role framework for modern HR professionals.

Design: The first D symbolizes the responsibility of HR professionals for designing core processes, systems and functions of Human Resource management such as Staffing, Training, Appraisal, Compensation & Job design. In addition the HR professionals have to assume the additional responsibilities for designing other associated frameworks of leadership, communication, team work, and inculcation of values, beliefs and ethics in the cultural fabric of the organization. It is worth mentioning at this stage that design of core or even ancillary frameworks of human resource management cannot be considered as emerging in a vacuum. HR professionals must anticipate in the process of design, how the present or future frameworks of HR are relating to different facets of the organization as well how these frameworks are geared for meeting the expectations of multiple stakeholders such as employees, customers and investors.

Develop: The second D symbolizes the role of being developers. It is essential that the modern HR professionals have to envision themselves as developers of employees and human resources. The most important asset for any organization is human resources, in this arena the responsibility of HR professionals is all the more significant because by developing frameworks of training, appraisal, compensation etc., HR people can help to improve the human capital pool of the organization and develop greater gradient of employee motivation and engagement. Developer's role does not restrict itself to the concept of employee training as HR professionals by developing human capital pool, motivating and empowering employees can also enable an organization to build further on its unique distinctive capabilities. HR professionals have a major responsibility in development of the cultural fabric of the organization and instilling values and beliefs that are in sync with the true identity of the organization.

Demonstrate: The third D symbolizes role of HR professionals as demonstrators.HR has emerged in a new role of being a closely integrated and strategic partner for the entire organization. If HR has to retain its new found position of prominence, then it is incumbent on HR professionals to demonstrate how HR systems, processes and functions relate positively to different facets of the organization. Demonstration responsibilities for HR professionals would include their ability to show tangible and perceptive linkages that HR practices can have with financial perspective, consumer perspective, business processes and frameworks of learning and growth for the entire organization.

Deliver: The last D relates to delivery of results. What is important for HR professionals is to see themselves in the role of deliverers of key competencies and capabilities for the organization. Demonstration of HR's linkage with areas of organizational performance is one thing, delivering results and living up to the expectations of the stakeholders is quite the other. Delivery of results should not only be restricted from perspective of employees but should encompass the crucial perspectives of consumers and investors also. If the company needs highly talented workforce then HR through development of selective staffing channels should deliver required results. If company needs inculcation of new knowledge, skills and abilities, then HR must deliver results by developing employee competencies through training. If the need for the organization is to elicit new type of behaviors then HR professionals have to take the lead for instilling new core values and beliefs in employees and in the overall mould of organizational culture.

In summation, it can be argued that HR today has emerged as an indispensable part and parcel of the modern organizations. Gone are the days, when for every recessionary trend HR department had to bear the first brunt or be the first victim to be guillotined. If companies today have to ensure their present or future viability and hope to hold on to their competitive edge, then HR must be given its due share of recognition and importance.

Useful Takeaways from Chapter

1. HR encompasses a range of activities under the rubric of employment relationship directed for attracting, retaining, developing and motivating employees.
2. HR serves by itself as a distinctive capability for the organization and is a source of other distinctive capabilities such as architecture, reputation and innovation.
3. HR is not just about people management but should be seen as a strategic business partner, an employee champion and a change agent for the entire organization.
4. HR is multidimensional and serves multiple stakeholders: employees, investors and customers.
5. HR management has to seen as an art form. One cannot have a "one size fits all" approach in dealing with HR issues.
6. HR frameworks can serve as a 360 degree lens for analyzing how HR relates to different aspects of organization and how these aspects in turn relate to HR.
7. Modern day HR professionals are Designers, Developers, Demonstrators and Deliverers of crucial capabilities and competencies for the organization.

CHAPTER 2

HR & Emotions

"Every employee is a finely tuned string of emotions. If management knows how to pluck the right strings then virtually nothing is impossible"

Fawziya Al Araimi

In my previous chapter, I have provided a generic understanding about HR, highlighted the growing importance of HR and outlined some of the major expectations from modern HR professionals. In this chapter, I would like to delve into an important but often neglected concept of Emotional Intelligence which quite often serves as the bedrock for management of human relationships. It can be noted that although emotional intelligence helps to define our very capacity for managing human relationships, very few books on HR actually delve into the important relationship that HR has with Emotional Intelligence. The goal of modern organizations should be to create "emotionally intelligent managers" who are receptive to the needs, expectations and emotions of modern day employees.

With the shift in focus of HRM practices from "Hard HRM" to "Soft HRM" the need for developing close psychological and emotional relationship between the employer and employees has become all the more necessary. After all if employees are to be visualized as the greatest assets for modern day companies then being sensitive to employee emotions, understanding, analyzing and connecting with employees across their emotional domain becomes a crucial necessity for improving overall organizational performance.

Importance of Emotions

It can be proudly proclaimed that we human beings are nothing but a bundle of emotions. Emotions represent us, shape us, make us and even have the capacity to break us. Emotions serve as a sophisticated system of internal guidance that can help us survive, develop and successfully compete. Emotions help us in making decisions as our feelings help us to make choices, help us in predicting and understanding behavioral responses in self and in others, facilitate in opening channels of communication, and enhance our capacity for relating to and connecting with each other. If emotions are so important then isn't it natural that we should be the in the driver seat for controlling and managing emotions, rather than letting emotions hijack our intellect, values and thinking. We should rule over emotions rather than allowing emotions to rule over us.

Human beings—Rational or Bundle of Emotions

I find it rather hilarious that importance of emotions is often neglected on the false pretext that man is a rational being. It is common knowledge that our actions and our decisions are influenced far more than our feelings and emotions than the cold logic of rationality alone. As the tumult of emotions unfolds within our bodies, intelligence is often forced to take a back seat. In light of the potency and power that emotions have over us in shaping our very existence, it seems natural to infer that all of us must learn the art of managing our emotions. Given the centrality of emotions in our lives, it should not come as a surprise that quotient for managing emotions (EQ) holds far greater sway than Quotient for intelligence (IQ) in defining human success. In fact it has been argued that 80% of our success is governed by EQ, while only 20% is attributable to IQ (Goleman, 1995).

Clearly if emotions play such a central part in our lives then identification and management of emotions should serve as a key ingredient in defining our capacity for management of relationships. It has been often argued that there is nothing more important for business success than the ability for developing productive workplace relationships (Goleman et.al, 2002). In the words of the eminent management Guru John Kotter it can be stated that the difficulty in management of workplace relationships sabotages more businesses than anything else. Failure of businesses should thus be seen more as a consequence of lack of understanding of emotions than as a consequence of poor strategic choices, design or planning frameworks. In light of the above, utilization of emotional intelligence(EQ) should be seen as a powerful tool for building relationships, predicting employee behavior, analyzing intentions, temperaments and motivation, gauging strengths and limitations in self and in others, and in lubricating networks of communication, teamwork and leadership.

Defining Emotional Intelligence—A universal necessity

So far, it becomes evident that emotions are important, but how do you manage and interpret emotions; and what is the concept of emotional intelligence? Mayer & Salovey (1997) define emotional intelligence (EQ) as the ability to monitor one's own and other's feelings, to discriminate amongst them and to use this information to guide one's own thinking and action. In other words the focus seems to be levied on sensing, understanding and effectively applying the power of human emotions for improving our ability to connect and relate to both self and others. From my perspective, I define emotional intelligence as encompassing "people skills and interpersonal intelligence" that helps in identification and management of emotions for personal and professional development and in improving our capacity for managing interpersonal relationships.

One thing that be easily gauged from all these definitions is that the language of emotions is something universal, so the necessity for managing of emotions should also be seen as a universal requirement. It does not matter whether you are a public sector official, a private sector manager, a banker, a consultant, an architect, a supervisor or even a CEO, your chances of success would be magnified many times over if you develop the dexterity in managing emotions for harnessing productive workplace relationships.

HR's leadership role in management of emotions

While I fully agree that managing emotions is a universal elixir for all professionals, nevertheless I am of the opinion that HR professionals can assume leadership in practicing, preaching and teaching the essential skills in management of emotions. HR professionals are entrusted with the key responsibility of being people managers, are assumed as employee champions for motivating and empowering employees. How can one possibly think of motivating, engaging or empowering employees without understanding the critical dimension of their emotions?

HR professionals act as employee champions, coaches, and mentors, therefore apart from practicing skills of emotional intelligence for themselves; they have to take on the responsibility of preaching, teaching, and training tenets of emotional intelligence for both employees and managers of the whole organization. After all we must bear in mind that emotional intelligence is very much a learnable skill and quite unlike IQ is not a fixed trait that cannot be improved upon (Goleman, 1998).

HR should assume leadership role in practice, training and management of emotional intelligence because:

1. HR is all about people management and EQ helps in motivating, engaging and empowering employees and managers.
2. Employees are just like bundle of emotions, HR is best informed on which strings to pull and when for improving performance and productivity.
3. HR helps to steer the winds of change, managing emotions is crucial for any successful change management initiative.
4. HR is responsible for building skills and competencies in employees; EQ is a learnable skill useful for managers and employees alike.
5. Ability to gauge emotions, relate and connect with employees is important for all core functions of HR be it staffing, training, appraisal, compensation or job design.
6. HR plays a stellar role in developing communication, team work and leadership frameworks, all of them require good EQ skills.

Models of Emotional Intelligence

Given the fact that HR should be in the driver's seat when it comes to practice and development of emotional intelligence skills, I would like to briefly outline two of the main models of emotional intelligence to highlight the conceptual tenets associated with management of emotions. It needs to be noted that while the concept of management of emotions has often been alluded to in many religious texts and treatises, nevertheless a formal analysis of models of emotional intelligence brings to the forefront the acknowledgement of power of emotions from a rational perspective. The two models I would briefly delve into are Mayer & Salovey

(Emotional Intelligence—Ability Model) and Goleman's model of Emotional Intelligence.

Mayer & Salovey model can be certainly considered as one of the oldest models of emotional intelligence propounded in the 1990s. It argues for 4 domains associated with emotional intelligence that are all inter related and iterative (Mayer & Salovey, 1997). Briefly the 4 domains associated with the model are:

1. Perception, Appraisal & Expression of emotions—this domain revolves around the ability to perceive and gauge emotions in self and in others and the ability to express and communicate these feelings.
2. Emotional Facilitation of Thinking: revolves around the ability to use emotions to direct attention, improve decision making and enhance cognitive processes.
3. Understanding & Analyzing Emotions: using knowledge of emotions for understanding both causes and consequences of emotions.
4. Management of Emotions—revolves around the capabilities for regulating self and other's emotions for promoting personal or social goals.

Goleman (1998) further popularized the concept of emotional intelligence by putting forth his own four domain model of emotional intelligence. The Goleman model of Emotional Intelligence arguably stretches beyond the interaction of emotions and mental thought by including the role and influence of social skills in relationship management. Goleman model also talks of 4 main domains for managing emotional intelligence, with two domains relating to personal competence (how we manage our self and our emotions) and the remaining two domains related to social competence(how we manage social awareness & relationships). The domains associated with Goleman's model are :

1. Self Awareness—Reading into our own emotions &
   recognizing its impact.
2. Self management—how we manage and control our
   own emotions
3. Social Awareness—how we empathize with others &
   are aware of social contexts.
4. Relationship management—how we use knowledge of
   emotions & social skills for improving relationships.

What needs to be noted is that one cannot think of superiority
of one model over the other. Each model has its own unique
strengths and limitations. The purpose is to see which one
works from our own unique perspectives either alone or in
combination and develop a unique game plan suiting our
individual requirements for managing emotions.

Practical Steps for managing Emotional Intelligence

Drawing out conceptual models of emotional intelligence
is one thing, creating practical frameworks for the art of
managing emotions is quite the other. The value of emotional
intelligence for modern day managers cannot be doubted,
but the confusion surrounds the way or the manner in which
management of emotions can be learned or practiced.
What needs to be realized is that emotional intelligence
is a learnable skill that can be learnt and improved upon,
however everyone has to develop his or her unique game
plan or road map in understanding how emotions can be
identified and effectively managed. The most important
ingredients in practicing art of management of emotions are
patience, flexibility, adaptability and experiential learning
to discriminate between what works and what does not work
from our individual perspectives.

The following is a brief list of 5 important steps that can aid
in management of emotions. While these steps lay down a
generic framework, every manager has to develop his or her

own specific game plan for practicing and learning the art of emotional intelligence.

Understand Yourself: The first step is to be self aware about your own emotions. Even Socrates had stated "Know Thyself". If one has to be good in managing relationships then the very first stepping stone is being familiar with oneself before even attempting to learn about others. Self awareness of emotions means that one must develop the ability to understand one's own emotions, how they impact us, how they influence our thinking and decision making.

Learn Management of your own Emotions: Being aware of our own emotions may be seen as the first step, but awareness of self emotions by itself holds little practical relevance unless we know how to manage these emotions. Once we become aware of what are emotions are, when and why they take place, we must also learn how we can influence and manage these emotions in ourselves. The main theme that resonates here is that we must learn how to rule over our emotions rather than letting emotions rule us. Self Management of emotions would involve not only displaying emotional self control—to keep away from disruptive emotions while simultaneously have the ability to harness the power of positive emotions. Being able to label emotions, cause or consequence of emotions is one part, having the ability to turn negative emotions into positive learning opportunities and deriving benefits from emotions is the more important other part. Self management of emotions would help us learn how to become more emotionally literate, how to control our emotions and mood swings, and how we can amplify our strengths and minimize our weaknesses.

Read, Interpret & relate to others: Self Awareness and management of our own emotions helps prepare the ground for analyzing and interpreting play of emotions in others. If any sort of relationship management has to be successful then we need to be not only in control of our own emotions but also inculcate within us the ability to effectively manage emotions in others. You need to put yourself in other people's shoes to understand how emotions can sway their decisions, feelings and cognitive processes. You need to empathize with others, feel what they feel and learn to sense the play of emotions from their unique perspectives. Reading and managing emotions in others would also necessitate being aware of the organizational context, what are the current trends and what type of organizational politics breeds within the organization.

Be aware of the crucial linking pins: An important detail that I would like to highlight is that at every level of transition especially when you are moving from awareness of emotions to the stage of management of emotions, you must be fully aware of the crucial linking pins. Awareness of emotions can only lead to effective management of emotions if you know the manner in which emotions can be used to facilitate thought, direct behavior and influence decision making. The focus is on being aware of causes and consequences of emotions, understand the relationship between emotions, thoughts, and human behavior.

Use power of soft skills in relationships: The final stage in the process is of course utilization of all our knowledge in identification, labeling and management of emotions for managing personal and professional relationships. The final frontier so to speak is relationship management. The power of productive work place relationships cannot be ignored as it is often the fundamental bedrock for defining organizational success. Being aware of emotions in ourselves and others, realizing how emotions influence our decisions and cognitive processes and how we can rule and control over emotions would all pave the way for effectively using our soft skills in managing employees. Soft skills such as leadership, developing others, communication, managing conflicts, building relational bonds and team work can all find new levels of effectiveness against the backdrop of our knowledge about emotions. Emphasis on soft skills alone in relationship management would not deliver the desired results unless the underpinning abilities are inculcated within us with regard to identification and management of emotions.

In summation, it can be noted that whether you want to be an inspirational leader, an employee champion, a change catalyst, your dexterity in handling and managing emotions would serve as your secret weapon for achieving personal and professional goals. There is no one best way of managing emotions; each of us needs to develop a unique game plan that works for us. The underlying criteria for emotional intelligence lies in our ability to understand and manage emotions in self and in others, and in our ability to harness the power of emotions for developing our strengths, connecting better with ourselves and others for creating productive and successful relationships in our personal and professional lives.

Useful Takeaways from Chapter

- Human beings are bundle of emotions. Emotions make us, shape us, represent us and even break us.
- Business failure should be seen more as a consequence of failing to understand and relate to employee emotions than as a consequence of faulty strategic choices.
- Emotional Intelligence deals with our ability for identifying and managing emotions for our personal, professional growth.
- HR can play a leading role both in practicing and in teaching tenets of emotional intelligence.
- Practical framework for practicing emotional intelligence would include: Understanding oneself & one's emotions, Relating to other's emotions, understanding the link pins between awareness & management of emotions, using power of EQ & Soft Skills in relationship management.
- Emotional intelligence is a learnable skill; therefore unlike IQ, it can be improved.
- There is no one best way for learning the art of managing emotions, develop your own unique game plan in view of your strengths & limitations.

CHAPTER 3

HR & STRATEGY

"Strategy does not mean taking a binocular to observe far away goal posts; it is about aligning all processes, systems and functions in accordance with overall organizational vision, mission and objectives"

Fawziya Al Araimi

It cannot be denied that the face of modern HR has remarkably been transformed. HR has now emerged as a business partner, a dedicated employee champion and a major change agent for the organization. All these new perspectives warrant investigating human resource management under the lens of overall organizational strategy of the firm. SHRM (Strategic Human Resource Management) is chiefly concerned about the manner in which HR strategy of the organization can be married or aligned with the overall business strategy of the firm to help gain competitive advantage, ensure long term profitability and sustainability of the firm.

Changing focus of HR to SHRM

The shift in focus to SHRM allows us to observe HR function as an integrated function for the entire organization, analyze HR processes in terms of the firm's overall competitive strategy and visualize expenditure on employees as an investment rather than as an expense. SHRM is clearly quite different from the assumptions associated with the traditional conceptualization of HR (Boxall & Purcell, 2003). First SHRM shifts the focus of HRM from focusing on individual performance to being responsible for the whole organizational performance. Second HR systems, processes and functions need to be looked as solutions for business problems of the organization and not just as solutions for employee problems of motivation, involvement and engagement.

A major impetus to the SHRM literature has been provided by the conceptual domain of Resource Based View of the firm, which argues that the real source of competitive advantage for any modern firm does not lie so much on the external factors of the firm, as on the internal resources and capabilities of the firm (Storey,2001). According to the Resource Based View of the firm, a firm can gain the much needed competitive advantage if its internal resources are rare, valuable, inimitable and non substitutable. There is a significant degree of agreement that human resources or a firm's employees are the most vital assets for any firm because the way human capital pool (knowledge, skills, abilities) is organized and the manner in which HR practices can form unique bundles, can all help in making the human resource function of the organization as rare, valuable, inimitable and non substitutable. In short, HR dimension of the organization can substantially account for its competitive advantage as articulated by resource based perspective of the firm.

The challenge of aligning HR strategy with the business strategy

So far it is clear that the birth of SHRM necessitates us to tie up strategically our HR strategy with the overall business strategy of the organization for ensuring viability and competitiveness of firms. But the pertinent question that arises is—how do we link labour management strategy with overall business strategy of the organization? Is there any simple way of doing so?

It may come as a surprise, but it is true, that there is no clear cut answer to these pertinent questions. We can tie labour management strategy with overall business strategy of the firm either based on "Best Practices" prescriptive framework or the "Best Fit" frameworks for the organization. While "Best Practice" school of thought advocates for adoption of a "universalistic approach" without paying attention to the organizational and the environmental contexts, on the other hand "Best Fit" practitioners argue for understanding ramifications associated with the specifics of the organizational context, as well as the development and maturity of the organization (Delery & Shaw, 2001).

Best Practice Perspective

The Best Practice way is simply based on a prescription of universalism. The task for HR department in linking their labour management to overall business strategy of the firm is therefore quite simply reduced to the identification and implementation of "universal best practice models" of HRM. All that the HR professionals have to be concerned about is identifying and judging "what is best practice available", choose the latest leading edge HR frameworks, and develop commitment and reward mechanisms for consistently embracing, adopting and implementing these frameworks.

It is common knowledge that based on years of research and successful track records of international companies that there are some clearly defined "best practice standards" which can be readily adopted. For instance everyone agrees that structured interviewing is far better than unstructured interviewing, behavior based performance appraisals are better than reliance only on trait based appraisals, result based measurement is more appropriate than only input based measurements, incentivization, training and autonomy can be universal tools for motivating and engaging employees in modern competitive environments. Many noted HR practitioners such as Pfeffer (1995) have produced elaborate list of effective best practices such as; employment security, employee ownership, high wages, team development, incentive pay, internal promotions, employee participation, information sharing, Job redesign, skill development, egalitarianism, regular feedback, and monitoring etc. On the face of it, all this looks too simple, just choose the prescribed successful best practice format, import it in your organization, apply it and get the results. However the reality is quite different. Just application of best practice bundles without paying any heed to specifics of organizational development or environmental parameters sound like a sure recipe for disaster.

Pitfalls of Best Practice

While Best Practice framework in general argues for enhancing the human capital pool of employees, focuses on motivating employees through incentive provision and employee ownership and promotes greater opportunities for employee participation and involvement, nevertheless it has its own share of pitfalls. Firstly in providing a general prescriptive framework of universalism for all companies, it ignores largely the unique organizational and environmental contexts that the companies may be operating under that may prevent the carte blanche transfer and adoption of these practices under the false assumption that one size would fit all.

Secondly the so called list of best practices is not well defined and different scholars have argued for different set of practices under the generic rubric of universalism. Which list should be adopted or which list should be ignored becomes a matter of pure conjecture and speculation. Moreover it may be stated that even in context of one umbrella organization, different units operating in different geographical locations may have different expectations, needs and requirements that a generic bundle of best practices model may fail to satiate in light of the differing cultural, environmental, economic and legal parameters that the same firm faces. Limitations with the Best Practice approach necessitate an examination of the alternative, which is the Best Fit perspective.

Best fit Perspective

Best fit perspective argues for the close integration of HR strategy with the business strategy or the competitive strategy of the firm by paying close attention to the organizational and environmental contexts that the firm operates in (Baron & Kreps, 1999). Each firm is unique and operates in its own domain wherein the specifics of organizational competitive strategy, stage of maturity and development of the organization would dictate how the alignment between HR and business strategy of the firm should take place.

There are two crucial aspects in this alignment. Firstly one has to be aware of the notion of vertical fit or external fit that speaks of tying the HR strategy of the firm with the overall organizational competitive strategy, stage of development or maturity of the firm. The second aspect is the concept of horizontal fit that argues for greater synchronization or positive bundling of HR systems so that individual HR practices can be seen as supporting, complimenting and coordinating with each other rather than being at loggerheads with one another (Boxall & Purcell, 2003). After all what good is vertical alignment of HR strategies, structures and systems if they conflict and contradict with each other internally? This would certainly vitiate the intent of alignment of HR with the overall business strategy of the firm.

Practical Steps for Best Fit Strategy (Vertical + Horizontal):

The following are few of the generic steps that can prove useful in bringing about the much needed vertical fit or external alignment between HR strategy, and overall organizational business strategy of the firm:

1. The first step is to understand carefully what is the Organizational Mission and Vision of the firm and what are the objectives for the firm that needs to be fulfilled. Such an examination would help to highlight why the firm exists, what are its priorities and how it wants to achieve these priorities.

2. The Second Step is to be aware of the overall business strategy of the firm and how elements within it are positioned. Overall business strategy is made up of competitive strategy, operations strategy, finance strategy and HR strategy of the firm. Through scanning of macro, micro external environments as well as the internal environment of the firm, one needs to understand how these interdependent elements align themselves for achieving the overall objectives of the firm.

3. The third step is to outline what would be the relevant employee behaviors for the firm in question, what are the expectations that the firm has in relation to their employees' behaviors, risk taking abilities, and nature and degree of teamwork expected from them. Moreover at this stage the firm should also develop an understanding of what are the expectations of the employees from the firm since the game of expectations should be seen as a two way street.

4. Understanding of employee behavior and expectations from employees would help us in outlining HR policies, practices, systems and structures that form part of overall HR strategy of the firm in coordination with the overall competitive and business strategy of the organization.

5. Institutionalization of relevant HR support practices in staffing, training & development, performance appraisal, compensation, Job design etc. should be made in order to further buttress the alignment of HR

strategy with overall organizational strategy of the firm.

6. All these steps would help us in receiving the desired HR outcomes by moulding employee behavior in close alignment with overall organizational goals, objectives and expectations.

It is evident from above steps that the vertical fit approach facilitates in an alignment of HR strategy with the overall business strategy of the organization and thus enhances the scope of HR function for contributing to the overall business framework of the organization. Moreover such strategic alignment of HR frameworks with the overall competitive strategy of the firm helps in recognition of the unique backdrop of organizational and environmental contexts that each firm operates in.

Vertical Fit needs to be balanced with a suitable Horizontal Fit

However what needs to be noted is that vertical alignment needs to be balanced by the horizontal alignment between different HR policies and systems so that the complementarities and synergies can be effectively realized. Horizontal Fit argues for designing of HR policies so that they can work in conjunction and in support of each other rather than acting as contradictory practices (Storey, 2001).

For example if the requirement of the firm is development of a creative workforce then highly selective recruitment and selection frameworks need to be supported with frameworks of training and development, greater autonomy and discretion, as well as a good, balanced system of compensation for rewarding creative behavior. Similarly if a company is looking for developing its team competencies then training and development should be focused on inculcating collective spirit and compensation frameworks should emphasize on rewarding display of collective behavior.

In essence therefore horizontal alignment of HR practices should be done is such a way so that individual HR policies, structures and systems work in unison for complimenting each other and developing greater overall synergy for the firm. However one needs to note that bundling of HR practices must adhere to some set standards or yardsticks of uniformity across the different departments of the organization (Baron & Kreps, 1999). It would make no sense if HR policies and norms fluctuated from one department of the organization to the other. Moreover it would look strange if alignment of such practices differentiated substantially across employee hierarchy within the organization or even across employees who are involved in doing the same type of work. Consistency should also be there in relation to the range of time period that the practices are instituted for. Just imagine how employees are going to react if they think that HR practices have no credibility as they keep on changing frequently.

Pitfalls of Best Fit

It is clear that "Best Fit" approach by focusing on alignment of HR strategy with the overall business strategy of the firm facilitates in treating HR as an integral component of the organization. Moreover by recognizing the organizational and environmental contexts that the firms operate in, it helps in aligning, designing and implementing HR strategies and policies that would be more relevant to the specifics of the organization and its general business landscape. However even the "Best fit" perspective has its own share of pitfalls.

Firstly linking HR strategy to overall business strategy of the firm is a complicated process as business strategy of a firm is composed of divergent interdependent elements such as competitive strategy, operations strategy, finance and HR strategy. It is difficult to understand how these interdependent elements would interact or resist each other.

Secondly the business landscape that companies operate in today is highly volatile and transient. With structural and systemic transformation taking place all the time, we cannot possibly think that one prescriptive alignment of HR strategy with firm's business strategy would remain stable for a long period of time. The emphasis therefore should be on developing in HR frameworks the quality of flexibility and adaptability so that we can develop competencies for unpredictable future.

Last but not least while alignment with business strategy helps in integration of HR function closely with the business dimension of the organization, nevertheless it cannot be ignored that HR as a multidimensional framework has responsibility towards consumers and employees and not just the business investors.

An approach of Collaboration and Balance: Given the merits and limitations associated with both Best Practice as well as Best Fit model, one needs to note that the best approach for moving forward should be based on collaboration and balance between these two models. While Best Practice standards help us in utilizing the leading edge of modern HR practices in areas of staffing, training, performance appraisal and compensation, nevertheless these practices cannot be adopted in a carte blanche manner without understanding their viability against the specific backdrop of the organizational and environmental contexts in which these practices are to be applied. In a similar way best fit helps in alignment of HR strategy with overall business strategy of the firm, nevertheless one must develop an understanding about how these specific practices weigh up or pan out against the industry prescribed "best practice benchmarks". Just because one adopts a "best fit perspective" does not mean that the company can become oblivious of the evolutionary or revolutionary best practice standards that may have emerged. After all it needs to be remembered that the greater the congruence is there between best fit and best practice standards, the easier it would be for the firm to develop its future competencies, plug in its weaknesses and strive more efficiently for gaining competitive advantage and improving overall profitability.

Useful Takeaways from Chapter

- Modern HR is a business partner, employee champion and a change agent.
- SHRM shifts the focus of HR to that of an integrated function, helps align HR strategy with that of the overall organizational business strategy.
- Strategic choices in labour management are important for competitive edge, viability and sustainability of modern firms.
- Resource Based View of the Firm has been instrumental in furthering the cause of SHRM.
- Best practice model advocates for universalism by embracing the leading edge HR practices without paying attention to unique organizational & environmental contexts.
- Best fit argues for aligning HR strategy with overall competitive strategy and acknowledges specifics of organizational and environmental contexts.
- Best Approach forward should be one of collaboration and balance between best practice and best fit models.

CHAPTER 4

RECRUITMENT & SELECTION

"If talented employees are like oxygen, then HR department functions as the lungs of the organization. HR helps to filter in oxygen as well as circulate it across the bloodstream of the organization"

Fawziya Al Araimi

Recruitment and Selection still remain one of the core responsibilities of HR department. HR professionals for many are seen as the hallowed gatekeepers of "talent" for the organization. If Human Resource is considered as the most vital asset for the organization, then it is the responsibility of HR professionals to see that the organization through its channels of recruitment and selection helps in attracting, retaining and motivating the right type of talented employees. It is well known that if you attract employees who are not talented you will only receive poor results and gaining of the much needed competitive edge would continue to remain a distant dream.

The marriage of the right employee with the right job through right recruitment and selection channels holds the magical key for future success, profitability and sustainability of modern organizations. Good recruitment and selection frameworks create high levels of motivation and commitment in employees, improve employee job satisfaction and performance, boost morale of workforce and reduce costs associated with labour turnover (Breaugh & Starke, 2000). Given that development of appropriate recruitment and selection frameworks are so important, the question often arises—what are the key features that recruitment and selection frameworks should have?

3 Salient Qualities of Recruitment & Selection Frameworks

I believe that any successful modern recruitment and selection frameworks must possess the following 3 main qualities or attributes:

1. **Efficiency:** Frameworks of recruitment and selection need to be efficient in delivery of the end results of improved performance, high workforce morale and improved job satisfaction. Methods utilized need to be fast, flexible, transparent and adaptable so that the right candidate gets recruited and selected.
2. **Equitability:** A fundamental necessity for all recruitment & selection frameworks is that of Equitability, Transparency and Fairness. Employees must feel the manner in which recruitment & selection is done in the company is transparent and just and it adheres to the highest principles of justice, fairness and ethics. This improves credibility of the company for both present and prospective employees. If prospective employees feel that the company has poor credibility in terms of its recruitment or selection channels then they would stay away from even applying to such firms.

Recruitment

Let me tackle these frameworks of recruitment and selection, one at a time. To begin with it is useful to note what is recruitment? At the very basic level recruitment can be seen as a process, function or activity that helps in generating a pool of applicants from which selection of right candidates can be made. In reality however, I feel that recruitment is far more than just a magnetic framework for attracting candidates. Recruitment should be concerned with attracting candidates, generating a pool of candidates as well maintaining the interest of the candidates in the organization (Barber, 1998). After all no point is served by just attracting candidates who waiver in their interest or commitment for joining the organization after being provided with the job offer.

The name of the game behind recruitment and selection is to attract, select and match the right candidate with the right job. It is not just a question of attracting and selecting the candidate but it is also concerned with fulfilling the expectations of the candidates to reduce turnover, employee attrition and improve employee commitment. After all what good does it serve if employees are recruited only to feel disillusioned later on and leave the organization as wilted, and drained out professionals.

5 Fundamental Questions in Recruitment:

Given the importance of recruitment in attracting the right type of potential candidate and in generating a pool of possible applicants, it can be noted that there are 5 fundamental questions that need to be successfully tackled for effective recruitment.

These are:

1. *Who/ What type of individual the organization wants to attract?*
2. *What is the level of knowledge, skills and abilities that the applicants must have?*
3. *What kind of message the organization wants to transmit across to potential candidates?*
4. *When or how the organization plans to start its recruitment processes?*
5. *Which are the sources that the organization should use for in recruiting candidates?*

It is clear that if the organization needs to be successful in its strategy for recruiting right type of candidates, it must endeavour to seek satisfactory answers for each of these questions. The answer to the first 3 questions can be provided by the processes of job analysis, job description and person specification. Question 4 regarding the timing and management of recruitment processes would be determined largely by the specific objectives of the firm, the vacancies available, the number and quality of applicants that organization wants to attract, and the type of diversity that the organization wants to promote. Question 5 can be answered through examination of some common internal or external sources of recruitment in light of the specific requirements and objectives of the firm.

Building the Foundation—Job Analysis, Job Description, and Person Specification:

One of the fundamental processes that forms the foundation for recruitment and selection frameworks is job analysis and its associated outcomes such as job description and person specification.

Job Analysis: Job analysis can be generically defined as the systematic process for identification of key features of the job for highlighting the standards against which recruitment and selection of candidates has to take place. Job analysis may take the form of task based analysis focusing on what specific tasks the job involves or behavior based analysis that focuses on behavioral expectations from employees as is common with managerial positions. Given the crucial role of job analysis, it needs to be carried out by HR department not in an isolated fashion but through a collaborative process of regularly interacting with concerned supervisors, managers and actual job holders. Techniques such as interactive interviews, observation diaries, checklists, critical incident methods can all facilitate in development of viable framework for Job Analysis.

Crucial Aspects that Job Analysis should focus on:

The following is a brief list of factors that should be considered for creating any job analysis framework:

1. Job Context: Be aware of the physical, social and cultural contours within which the job is to be performed.
2. Mental processes: Understand the type of mental and cognitive processes that are required. Focus on the knowledge, skills and abilities required.
3. Work Output: Understand the physical activities required for the job and the tools and equipments.
4. Information Frameworks: Analyze what the information frameworks that workers would use for receiving and transmitting information.
5. Relationship Matrix: Understand the network of relationships that the job incumbent has to interact with in performing his duties. Who is the worker reporting to, who would report to the worker etc?

Job Description: Job description is one of the critical outcomes of job analysis. It focuses on highlighting what is the nature, content, scope and responsibilities associated with the job. A good job description therefore should be written in a simple and direct manner that underlines:

The main purpose of the job—What the job is all about?

Main tasks or Behaviours—What the main tasks? What are the main behavioral expectations?

Key Responsibilities—What are the key responsibilities associated with the job?

Scope of Job—What is the nature, content and scope of job?

Relevance—What is the level of relevance of the job for the organization? The number of people that need to be supervised or the command chain.

Person Specification/ Person Profile: Another associated outcome of job analysis, along with Job Description is the Person Specification or the Person Profile. This helps in outlining a brief profile of the potential "ideal candidate" so that the connection between the right person and the right job can be made. A good Person Specification or Person Profile would highlight:

- The level of knowledge, skills and abilities required.
- The experiential knowledge required.
- The Qualifications and training that the employee should possess.
- Personal Qualities & Traits that the organization is looking for.

In short the both the Job Description & Person specification frameworks help to prepare the groundwork for the recruitment & selection process to unfold. A well crafted job analysis and person profile would be helpful in attracting a more specific, narrower pool of job applicants who can potentially fit well with the expectations of the company.

Importance of transmitting realistic and credible information to applicants:

An important point to note is that recruitment & selection should be based on transmitting realistic and credible information to potential applicants. The information conveyed to potential applicants should be transmitted in a clear and direct manner so that future employees don't just join the bandwagon of the organization riding on the wave of unrealistic expectations. After all the goal of recruitment and selection is to attract and select the right candidate for the right job, not just in attracting candidates who would come to the organization with unrealistic expectations or leave later on as disgruntled former employees. In this regard Realistic Job previews can be used as a simple yet powerful tool for dissemination of credible information.

Realistic Job Previews: Realistic Job Previews provided in form of videos, web pages or booklets can facilitate self selection in employees for applying to jobs, can create better transparency and balance between organizational and employee expectations, improve chances of job acceptance, and reduce future employee attrition or turnover rates (Breaugh & Starke,2000).

Timing the Recruitment Cycle:

It is important for the organization to appropriately time the framework of recruitment to understand when the process of recruitment should start and when should it finish. Job analysis and associated results such as Job Description and Person Specification are all predicated on the belief that a job exists, it is stable and it is possible for identifying categorically the nature, content and scope of the job. HR department has to play a leading role in close consultation with other departments and managers in creating a planned time framework for recruitment & selection processes. They have to identify the needs of the organization in relation to specific jobs, the actual number of jobs that would need to filled, the time cycle pattern of jobs in light of promotion, employee turnover, and attrition rates, the cost and speed of filling jobs and the ratio of offers to acceptance. Moreover timing of recruitment activities need to be organized depending on what are the best possible time periods available for attracting pool of candidates from career fairs or at universities or schools.

Identifying the Right Sources for Recruitment:

Recruitment is not just concerned with attracting candidates but focuses on attracting a pool of right candidates for facilitating selection. Sources of recruitment can therefore be instrumental in determining the number, type and quality of applicants who would be applying for the job openings. There is no rule of thumb in determining which source of recruitment is most ideal, rather depending on the nature, content and scope of job, identification of sources of recruitment should be made. A brief list of possible sources is presented below:

Internal vs External Sources: One of the first decisions is to identify whether recruitment needs can be catered to from inside the organization or from outside the organization. Internal sources of recruitment can be valuable if employees already possess the requisite knowledge, skills, abilities and experience for the job. Internal sources of recruitment can lead to enhancing employee scope of jobs; facilitate in greater motivation, loyalty and involvement of employees. On the other hand if employees possessing knowledge, skills and abilities need to be sourced from outside then external sources of recruitment should be utilized. External sources of recruitment help in beefing up the potential employee data base for even future cycles of recruitment by generating a large number of potential candidates for the ever expanding database of the organization.

Newspapers & Journals: Newspapers and journals are another viable source for external recruitment. While Newspaper advertising may be a bit expensive, nevertheless these can be successful in generating a large number of potential candidates due to their geographical coverage. Journals on the other hand can be used for sourcing in targeted candidates for senior executive level positions.

Manpower Agencies & Job Centres: Manpower agencies and job centers are particularly useful for lower level administrative jobs that are largely task based.

Specialist Executive Search Organizations: These can be useful for sourcing in candidates for executive level positions as they have readily available data bases of potential candidates, however these can turn out to be expensive. Care should be taken that these organizations are credible as they would be representing the initial face of the organization.

Universities/ Colleges & Schools: These can be particularly useful for generating a large number of potential candidates especially for entry level jobs. Moreover participation in career fairs of these institutions also helps in creating a better brand image for the organization and facilitates in creating a greater awareness about the organization.

Internet: Internet provides a highly cost effective source of recruitment. Companies can advertise directly job openings in their own website, seek help of professional job portals or even create a special job board for its job openings with interactive interface. However reach of internet is restricted to only computer literate population, and may not be a viable option for countries with low internet penetration or computer literacy rates.

Direct Applications & Employee Referrals (Informal Sources): Direct applications help to build up a contingency data base for future recruitment needs of the organization. Employee referrals are very effective as these have already undergone an informal screening phase from the perspective of the referring employee. Moreover the potential candidate is also benefited as he also receives a realistic job preview about the job from the referee employee that can facilitate in creating realistic expectations.

Selection Frameworks

Selection should be seen as "cherry picking", picking the "best" from the given pool. Recruitment on the other hand must ensure that the basket is filled with only cherries. It needs to be noted that while recruitment has at its heart attracting and generating a pool of potentially right candidates, selection forms the vital framework for selecting the right candidate for matching him or her to the job. Whether jobs are created to fit employees or employees are selected to fit jobs, the emphasis of selection mechanisms is to pick the best possible candidates who can enhance organizational performance, productivity and employee morale (Saldago, 1999). If Human resources are considered the most valuable assets, then selection frameworks ensure the selection of the right resources for the organizational bandwagon. Employees through their shared values, beliefs and assumptions also form a crucial part of organizational cultural dynamics; therefore the "right employee" should be selected on the basis of his ability to gel well with the organizational culture and the overarching philosophy, vision and mission of the organization.

Some Well Known Tools for Employee Selection:

The following is a brief list of the tools that can be used in the selection process. It needs to be noted that choice of specific selection tools would vary across companies depending on what type, level and qualifications they are looking for in candidates as well as what are the specific requirements of the job for which selection is being made.

Application Forms–These are useful as a prescreening tool for initial sifting of potential candidates. Designing of application forms should be straightforward and realistic so that it acts like a window for giving first hand information about the prospective candidate, qualification, relevant experience, knowledge, skill level and specific abilities. Application forms can serve as an initial benchmark for short listing of candidates in a quick and cost effective manner. Care needs to be taken to ensure safety and confidentiality of the database in keeping with data protection legal requirements and stipulations.

Biodata : Another useful tool for selecting employees that can often be used in conjunction with the CV. Biodata often takes the form of an extended questionnaire having multiple choice questionnaire formats that can be appropriately weighted and scored according to employer's needs and requirements. Bio data information can provide useful insights about applicant's personal information, education, qualifications, employment experience, and other related traits and competencies.

References & Background Checks: Effective tools for checking the background of applicants as well as the veracity of their qualifications, skills and professional experience. Always focus on checking at least two professional references. This helps in getting vital insights about the candidate from their previous employer's perspective or from the perspective of nominated referees. Additionally confidential background checks about criminal history, credit record, and relevant personal dispositions of employees can also be made in conjunction with the forwarded references.

Psychometric & Psychological Tests: Useful tool in assessing candidate's crucial facets such as personality, intelligence(EQ & IQ), sense of reasoning, problem solving, interpersonal skills and decision making acumen. However these tests must be used as a supplementary tool and not as a primary tool because of inherent subjective discrepancies that might creep in as well as the generic shortcomings associated with developing appropriate psychometric yardsticks.

Assessment Centers: Assessment centers employ a variety of techniques for testing potential applicants across different domains of cognitive skills, interpersonal skills, cognitive reasoning, team work etc. Often these centers focus on engaging the applicants in some sort of role play and group work activities so that their abilities in team work, decision making and logical reasoning can be gauged through practical demonstration. Assessment centers however are mostly used by large corporations and involve some degree of investment, although its usefulness as an initial sifting framework cannot be doubted.

Work Samples: By analyzing previous samples of work, companies can gain the much needed insights into professional competence of the employee in his or her chosen field. Work samples can be used as effective evidence for analyzing both task based as well as behavior based competencies of prospective employees.

Interviews—The Numero Uno Tool for Selecting Employees:

Interviews can be easily seen as the numero uno tool for selecting the right candidate. Interviews provide the selectors the opportunity to interact face to face with the potential applicant for understanding his/ her level of skills, competencies, knowledge and professional expertise. Interviews help to gauge whether the applicant is the "most suitable candidate for the job" as well as analyze how he performs in relation to other competing applicants. From the perspective of applicants, interviews provide the applicant with the opportunity to understand more thoroughly the organization, as well ask relevant questions pertaining to the job or the company. Interviews thus offer an interactive platform through which companies can analyze the suitability of the candidate and applicants can analyze the suitability of the job or the company in light of their preconceived expectations.

Interviews are highly flexible selection tool and can be delivered in a variety of formats—formal interviews/ informal interviews, one to one interviews/ panel interviews, structured or unstructured. The choice of specific interview format would largely depend on the individual preferences of the company, the type and level of job applied for, and the time frame available for making the selection. Generally for lower level positions, single interview is sufficient, however for managerial and senior executive level positions, a series of interviews in the individual or panel interview format is highly recommended.

From the experience of HR professionals, it can often be inferred that interviews should be created either on the structured format or at least in the semi structured format. Structured or semi structured interviews prove effective as they provide a roadmap for guiding the interview discussion, serve as a useful benchmark tool against which all candidates can be tested, and reduce subjective variations in the framing of questions by testing all applicants on the same type and level of questions.

15 Useful Tips for Conducting Interviews:

1. Always familiarize yourself with the background of the candidate prior to interview.
2. Preplan a framework of questions to be asked and anticipate what questions candidates might pose.
3. Use similar structure for all applicants to make the selection process transparent.

4. Agree upon a scoring scale for measuring specific areas relevant for the job.
5. Chalk out or distribute questions amongst interviewers prior to interview.
6. Chalk out a tentative time frame that each interview should last for.
7. Always greet the candidate and make the candidate feel comfortable by asking one or two generic questions. Idea is to select the best candidate and not rule out talented but nervous candidates.
8. Ask specific job related questions. Refrain from asking personal questions.
9. Ask candidates about specific professional situations faced, what tasks they were entrusted with, and what were the results achieved.
10. Don't forget or ignore the questions posed by candidates.
11. Make sure that the candidate becomes familiar with the terms and conditions of the job.
12. Apprise the candidate about the procedure of selection.
13. Inform the candidate about the response time of possible decision.
14. Take careful notes during the interview process to reduce reliance on memory and for proper comparison in post interview discussions.
15. Assure the candidate of complete confidentiality with all the data presented.

Useful Takeaways from Chapter

- Recruitment & Selection still remain key responsibilities of HR department.
- HR professionals still are seen as gatekeepers of talent for the organization.
- Good recruitment & selection are essential for motivating employees, improving commitment and overall performance of organization.
- Modern Recruitment & Selection frameworks should always be Effective, Efficient and Equitable.
- Recruitment is defined as the process of attracting applicants, maintaining their interest and influencing their job choices.
- 5 fundamental questions in recruitment are: Who is to be attracted? What knowledge, skills and abilities are required? What kind of message should be transmitted, what should be the timing of recruitment process, and which sources of recruitment are to be used?
- Job Analysis, Job Description and Person Specification form the basic foundation for any recruitment & selection process.
- Realistic Job Previews can help in removing misconceptions.
- Sources of recruitment can be informal such as direct applications, employee referrals or formal such as newspapers, journals, magazines, recruitment agencies, job centers etc.
- Selection is chiefly concerned with picking the best cherry from the basket of cherries.
- Some of the tools for selection are: application forms, biodata, references & background checks, assessment centers, psychometric tests etc.
- Interviews still remain the numero uno tool for selecting employees.

CHAPTER 5

Training & Development

> "There is nothing that training cannot do. Nothing is above its reach. It can turn bad morals to good; it can destroy bad principles and recreate good ones; it can lift men to angelship".

> Mark Twain

Training and development is basically concerned with imparting of knowledge, skills and abilities as well as the creation of learning and growth opportunities for professional and personal development of employees. If human resources are to be seen as the most important assets for an organization then it is natural to assume that companies need to invest in developing the potential and capabilities of their employees. If HR professionals see themselves as employee champions, then they have to assume leadership role in training and development of employees. Training & development functions can serve as the primary source for gaining competitive advantage as they help in not only improving organizational performance and productivity but also improve levels of employee retention, motivation, and morale (Keep, 1989). Whether companies want to improve human capital pool, motivate or empower workers, or change employee attitudes; in every domain paradigm of training has its own special place of importance.

Benefits of Training & Development:

I have always visualized training as a multidimensional tool that showers benefits on all the stakeholders of the organization. Training function can be seen as satisfying the divergent needs of the "holy trinity" of any organization i.e the needs of the investors, the employees and the consumers. High levels of training often translate into generating higher quality in products, create better standards in service and account for higher levels of consumer satisfaction. Employees who are well trained often display higher gradient of motivation, organizational commitment and loyalty. Investors benefit as trained employees help in achieving higher productivity for the whole organization through improved efficiency and cost effective utilization of present resources. In short training showers multifaceted advantages for both organization and employees.

It may be interesting to note that investment in training can be likened to investment in a love relationship; the more you put in, the greater would be the dividends received, and the sweeter would be the bond of relationship between management and employees.

The table below briefly highlights some of the benefits of training for the individual employees as well as for the organization as a whole.

Training Benefits for Employees	Training Benefits for Organization
<ul><li>Higher KSA</li><li>Better cognitive skills</li><li>Higher efficiency</li><li>Higher motivation</li><li>Better commitment</li><li>Employee empowerment</li><li>Greater loyalty</li><li>Lower labor turnover</li><li>Job Satisfaction</li><li>Positive employee attitude</li></ul>	<ul><li>Competitive Advantage</li><li>Better performance</li><li>Higher productivity</li><li>Loyal workforce</li><li>Consumer Satisfaction</li><li>Better Quality & Service</li><li>Better labour relations</li><li>Lower worker turnover</li></ul>

Training & Development: Think of it as a composite Package:

While there are some commonalities between these two paradigms, nevertheless there are significant differences in relation to their focus, scope and time frame. Training can be seen as focusing narrowly on the competencies required for the job and the time frame involved is limited. Development on the other hand goes beyond the narrow domain of job competencies and focuses on creating long term learning and growth opportunities for employees. In the words of the eminent Leadership Guru John Maxwell, training has the potential to change performance, whereas development can change lives. Therefore it is important for companies to look at training and development as a composite package, as emphasis on training alone would not create significant impact on lives of employees.

5 Key Objectives of Training & Development:

Given the multiple benefits that accrue to training and development, it is essential for virtually all organizations to be clear about what should be the key aims and objectives of their training and development programs. It is common knowledge that organizations that do not have a well defined framework of aims and objectives for designing, developing, implementing and evaluating training often end up as losers in the competitive race of modern times. The following are the 5 main key objectives that any training and development program should focus on achieving:

1. Training & Development programs should be created so that the organization becomes efficient and sustainable.
2. Focus should be on not only identifying the skill gap but also on outlining the possible roadmap for bridging the gap.
3. Training and Development processes should be seen as a major source for gaining competitive advantage as it caters to the needs of the "holy trinity"; consumers, investors and employees.
4. Training & Development should ultimately focus on impacting and changing workers' lives, help employees to move up their individual or collective learning curves.
5. Training should focus on improvement of employee morale, employee motivation as well as focus on increasing efficiency in internal and external processes of the organization.

5 Essential Ingredients for any Training & Development Programs:

Clearly if training is such an important facet for the organization, then it is important to note what should be the composition of these training & development programs? While it can be recognized that every training package has to be unique in some form or the other in light of the specific needs and requirements of individual firms, nevertheless there are some common key elements that every training package must have. The key ingredients that must be there in any training package are:

- **Hard & Soft Skills**—Every training package ultimately aims to rectify the skill gap in the employees, so every training package must have an input of hard and soft skills. Hard Skills are those that have clear objectives, can be measured and essentially necessary for job completion such as computer knowledge, product related competencies, machine handling & repairing skills etc. On the other soft skills are more concerned with individual personal development and growth. Communication, empathy, leadership, creative thinking, interpersonal skills etc. are all examples of soft skills. Development of both skills is deemed essential for overall organizational success, without hard skills one cannot perform in the job and without soft skills one can't develop the acumen in employees for understanding, working and relating to each other.
- **Conceptual Knowledge & Education**: Every type of training and development package must include knowledge that also encapsulates some general principles of education for broadening the horizon of employees. Employees must have general awareness about basic principles of management, business operations, human relations, industry or sector specific information. Understanding generic principles related

to education can play a vital part in personal growth and development of employees.

- **Rational logic & Problem Solving:** Every training & development program should utilize effective frameworks of rational logic and decision making. Main idea behind training is fostering of efficiency & creative thinking, both of which require understanding of logic & rationality. Imparting of problem solving skills to employees would enable employees to collect and analyse relevant data from new perspectives for devising creative out of the box solutions. Good logic & problem solving abilities can serve as bedrock for gaining competitive advantage and improved productivity for modern firms (Hayes & Stuart, 1996).

- **Motivation & Attitude Development:** Training packages can also be seen as source of motivation and empowerment for workers. Therefore every training package must focus in line with the overarching organizational philosophy how positive values, beliefs and assumptions can be created in employees. Employees need to develop positive attitudes for reducing their inbuilt resistance and efficiently adapting to the winds of change (Grugulis,2007).

- **Moral Dimension:** No Training & Development can be considered complete unless it inculcates the much needed moral dimension in employees. Companies today do not just focus on their narrow bottom line but on their broader responsibilities towards consumers, community, society and the environment. Ethical behavior in employees' conduct is a quintessential necessity for modern organizations. Therefore all training and development packages must have a dose of morality and ethics ingrained in them for making employees discharge their responsibilities in an ethical and responsible manner.

Identification of options for training:

A key responsibility of HR professionals as well as the senior managers in the organization is to identify what are the possible options of training, and which option should be chosen? This certainly requires a careful investigation into what the training needs of the organization are, what are the type of skill gaps that need to be rectified, what are the kind of available resources and how effectively these resources can be optimally utilized. The generic options of training are presented below, though it must be remembered that every organization would develop its own unique game plan about how these options would be used either in isolation or in conjunction.

Internal Training Programs: Internal training programs are developed by the internal training department. Most of the large organizations have their internal training departments with dedicated specialist trainers from the HR section or other relevant departments. The effectiveness of these internal training programs would largely depend on the caliber and competency of the internal training staff, the kind of expertise and experience they have in imparting training, and the kind of resources that are available for providing training in accordance with industry prescribed "best standards". Advantage of having internal training departments is that the dedicated trainers of the organization are well aware of the specific individual and collective needs of the employees and are familiar with their dispositions, preferences and cultural beliefs. Furthermore internal training departments can always utilize generic best practice manuals and successfully adapt these to suit the specific needs and requirements of the organization. However creating and maintaining a large internal training department with a large data base of training packages calls for considerable expenditure.

External Trainers/ In-house Programs: Given the rapid pace of change that modern organizations face, companies may require the assistance of specialist external trainers who can more effectively bridge the skill gaps of the employees. If employees need to be trained in new areas then resorting to external trainers is a viable option. In such cases it is necessary for the HR department to develop a list of new competencies, skills and abilities required by employees or requested by departments and then seek out proactively the external trainers who can deliver the goods. HR department can liaise with trainer agencies, employer associations, trade magazines, chambers of commerce registered data base of certified trainers or established trainers from colleges and university to satiate their needs. To make it cost effective special contracts can be drawn based on hourly rates or number of employees or through utilization of existing in house training facilities.

Commercial Training Establishments: There is also the option of seeking specialized training classes for employees from commercial training vendor establishments. In these cases it is important for HR professional to make an exhaustive list of commercial training vendor establishments that are operating within their region. It is highly recommended that before a commercial training vendor is selected, some key questions need to satisfactorily answered such as what training packages are being offered? Would these meet with specific requirements of the company? What is the range of prices offered? What is the previous level of satisfaction with such programs? What value additions can such programs bring in for the company? Can long term tie ups be facilitated etc?

E Learning Platforms: ICT revolution has brought to the forefront usage of E Learning platforms for training and developing employees. In general E learning frameworks can be used effectively in two ways. Firstly the companies can create their own E learning platforms that can serve as an interactive framework for training and developing their employees in basic technical or task based skills. Secondly E learning vendor establishments can be contacted for delivering specific bespoke training packages in view of the unique needs of the organization. Care should be taken to find out how user friendly these product offerings are and how effective follow up and employee evaluation tools are there with each of the product offerings so that a balanced decision can be taken for investing in these programs.

Universities/ Colleges/ Schools: Universities, Schools and Colleges are another viable option for training. It is common for companies today to create tie ups with established local, regional or international universities for training and educating their employees. With training being progressively viewed as an investment, many modern corporations choose to collaborate with universities & colleges for sponsoring their employees for short term or long term courses. Fostering of close ties with universities, schools and collegiate institutions ensures that employees would remain aware of the cutting edge in scientific and technological fields as well as receive opportunities for personal and professional growth.

Planning an effective framework for Training:

There is nothing more important in the field of training than developing or designing a proper framework for training and development. Training & development of employees requires substantial investment on part of the companies, therefore it is imperative that the companies must carefully plan and develop a framework for training so that their organization objectives are effectively met (Heyes & Stuart, 1996). Rushing into or adopting a training package without developing a framework for training is a recipe for sure disaster. Listed below are some of the generic steps that can prove useful in developing and designing frameworks of training :

- **Training Needs Analysis**—The first and perhaps the most important process is conducting a proper training needs analysis (TNA). An effective training need analysis would help in diagnosing not only the pertinent present problems but also the future challenges facing the company. Training needs assessment can be carried out across two levels: at the level of the individual or at the level of the group. The focus of investigation in both these cases is on identification of the level of knowledge; skills and abilities of the workforce, identification of the critical skill gaps, and highlighting the areas that need improvement. Identification of knowledge, skills and abilities in case of individual employees can be made through methods such as questionnaires, interviews, attitude surveys, work samples etc. At the group level skill set identification can be made in relation to organizational objectives, work planning systems, efficiency indices, customer feedbacks and collective interviews. Job Analysis, job description and person specification profile made by HR department during recruitment phase can also serve as a useful starting point.
- **Developing the Instructional Objectives**: The second part of the process is associated with developing the instructional objectives. These form a useful benchmark for focusing on what the key abilities that the employees must develop as well as in creating a comparative framework to evaluate how the objectives have been met. Instructional objectives therefore serve as a reference point to analyze what the focus of training and development should be and also as a judgment framework to gauge if the results delivered match up with the expectations.
- **Composition of Training & Development:** Having outlined the instructional objectives, the next stage is to understand what the composition of training program should be? In other words we need to focus on what are the essential inputs required for developing

specific training programs. The decision about what goes into the training programs needs to be taken at a collaborative level through close consultation and interaction between HR professionals and concerned department heads or managers. Some key questions that need to be answered are: Should the training focus on development of hard skills or soft skills or both? How much of conceptual knowledge and techniques should be taught to employees? Are we looking only on narrowly fulfilling skill gap requirements or preparing employees for anticipated skills for future contingencies? What kind of moral and ethical inputs one should ingrain in the particular training? Etc.

- **Inclusion of Learning Mechanisms:** It goes without saying that learning should be a crucial component of any training program. What good would it be to have employees trained if they do not develop the ability to learn or develop themselves? We need to understand that employees are adults and therefore training delivered to them should be in tune with the Kolb's prescription of learning cycle, wherein employees assimilate and learn by passing through 4 different stages of learning such as concrete experience, reflective observation, abstract conceptualization and active experimentation (Kolb, 1986). In any training program there must be some profusion of principles of learning such as outlining of goals, practical experience, scheduled format of instruction, reinforcement, and feedback mechanisms so that employees absorb and retain what they are being taught. After all no purpose would be served if employees were to forget the majority of what they are being trained. Training that does not create suitable retention in employees is similar to chucking money into a deep pit where there is no chance of recovering it.

- **Exploring the options for delivering training:** A careful investigation needs to be carried out about the internal capabilities of the organization and the type of competencies that internal trainers possess so that decision can be made whether training can be delivered from within the organization or it has to be sourced from outside. We need to analyse whether the instruction of training can be best delivered in instructor led format or self paced learning format. The delivery style should it be in the form of lectures, demonstrations or simulation training. Analysis should also be made about whether this kind of training should be part of OJT(on job training) framework or do employees need to be trained off the job. A thorough cost benefit analysis should be made about several available options such as internal training, external trainers, E Learning options, and commercial training vendors before any investment decision is made.

- **Monitoring of Results:** Ultimately no designing of training and development can be complete without accounting for how the results of training would be monitored or measured. After all the start of training design through training needs analysis was predicated on the belief that there are some clear objectives for which training needs to be delivered. Every training program needs to be analyzed ultimately in relation to how successful it was in achieving its intended objectives. This would facilitate in laying the roadmap of how future improvements or changes should be accommodated in the training and development programs of the organization.

Evaluation of Training & Development:

It goes without saying that the ultimate name of the game in training is evaluation of results. Training employees is an expensive business and organizations only engage in it based on the conviction that it would provide ample benefits and returns. Training needs analysis helps to outline the crucial objectives for developing training programs, evaluation of training helps in understanding how these objectives have been realized. Evaluation is all about monitoring of results and making a thorough cost benefit analysis of the investments made and the results delivered or gained.

Given the importance of evaluation, it is clear that organization evaluation specialists must have clear prescribed objectives against which they have to measure the success of training programs. Evaluation cannot be seen as a piecemeal process; rather it needs to be observed as a continuous and integrated process with design, delivery, implementation, and institutionalization of training programs (Heyes & Stuart, 1996). HR professionals need to delineate clearly the target dates for phases of evaluation process and collect, analyze and interpret data from employees regarding the efficacy, efficiency and viability of the training programs.

Some Key Questions related for Evaluation that need to be answered are:

- What were the objectives of the training program and have these been achieved?
- Has the training program been successful in delivering the intended knowledge, skills and abilities to employees?
- Has the training program been successfully in bridging the skills gap?
- Do the benefits outweigh the costs involved?
- What has been the level of learning associated with the training program?
- Has the training improved performance and efficiency of employees?
- Can the employees successfully transfer their newly learnt skills to their jobs?
- Can the training program prove useful for other departments?
- Should these programs be conducted in future also?
- How can further improvements be created in the present fold of training program?

Some Common Tools for Evaluation:

- **Employee Surveys & Questionnaires**—Useful tool as these can be conducted during the pre and post training sessions. Such surveys and questionnaires can help in understanding the efficacy and validity of training programs as gauged from perspective of employees.
- **Control Groups**—Employees can be divided into groups, those that are exposed to training and those who are not. Comparative analysis can be created to find out the effectiveness of training programs in relation to control groups.
- **Longitudinal Studies**—Longitudinal or time series analysis can be made by collecting and analyzing relevant data from employees at different points of time. This would help to show whether training principles are being translated in actual job contexts and how the employees perceive the effectiveness of training programs at different points of time.

Useful Takeaways from Chapter

- Training & development is concerned with imparting of skills and providing of career opportunities for growth and development.
- HR as employee champions should assume leadership in training and developing employees.
- Training & development showers benefits for the "holy trinity" of stakeholders: consumers, investors and employees all benefit.
- Training & development can act as a source of competitive advantage, help firms to be more productive and make workers more motivated.
- Training & development should go hand in hand as a composite framework.
- Training composition should include a potpourri of hard skills, soft skills, educational concepts, rational logic & problem solving tools.
- Companies can choose from several training delivery options such as: internal trainers, external trainers, commercial training vendors, etc.
- Effective Framework design for training is essential given the substantial investment that training entails.
- Evaluation of training & development should be done in a continuous manner.

CHAPTER 6

PERFORMANCE APPRAISAL

"Performance is the critical factor that separates
success from failure. Appraising performance is
like connecting with the heart and the mind of
the organization".

Fawziya Al Araimi

Probably there are very few things more important for the
organization than developing a well defined system for
appraising performance. Performance appraisal (PA) can
be counted amongst the most crucial functions of modern
HR professionals that can help in gauging the net worth of
employees, identify their present levels of performance and
outline a road map for utilizing their full potential. Well
defined performance appraisal systems can improve the
productivity of organizations, engender better employee
motivation, serve as a basis for training employees, and form
the foundation for rewarding & compensating employees
(Fisher & Thomas, 1982).

In short, I find performance appraisal to be a multidimensional
tool that can record employee performance, determine
employee reward structures, facilitate in decisions regarding
promotions, demotions or termination, identify skills gaps
and create the foundation for future training and career
development. It has often been stated that the ability for

correctly interpreting performance helps in making the vital distinction between organizational success and failure.

Defining Performance Appraisal: Simple or Complex:

Quite simply, performance appraisal needs to be seen as a process that helps in the identification, observation, measurement and development of human performance (Fletcher, 2001). The first component of this process is concerned with identification of factors or criteria that define organizational performance. The second aspect is that these identified factors or criteria should be observable so that fair and honest assessment can be made. If the criteria are observable then these can be measured and evaluated. If proper measurement and evaluation can be made then we can understand how improvement can be generated so that the present and future competencies of the organization can be holistically improved. What needs to be noted is that in all these processes we need to be concerned not only about the nature, content and the manner in which performance appraisal would be carried out but also the context in which performance appraisal takes place (Roe, 1999).

Interestingly, it can be observed that while appraising performance on the face of it looks like a highly scientific and objective process, nevertheless the subjective dimension associated with appraising performance cannot be ignored. We cannot overlook the high level of subjectivity that can inadvertently creep in any performance appraisal system on account of problems associated with defining objective criteria or receiving impartial and fair appraisals from supervisors. The challenge therefore is to minimize subjectivity and improve objectivity for improving the accuracy and fairness of any form of performance appraisal system.

Benefits of Performance Appraisal:

Whatever be the challenges or drawbacks associated with measuring performance, it cannot be denied that performance appraisal remains a key organizational process that provides multiple benefits:

- Performance Appraisal (PA) can act as a major source in developing competitive advantage.
- Performance appraisal helps in recording, monitoring, evaluating and developing human performance.
- PA can account for improving overall organizational productivity.
- PA helps in identifying the skill gaps in employees and identifies development needs of employees.
- PA can serve as a benchmark for future recruitment & selection frameworks of the organization.
- PA helps in making crucial decisions regarding promotion, demotion, termination or transfer of employees.
- PA serves as a basis for developing compensation & reward frameworks.
- PA helps in improvement of customer satisfaction by making employees more responsive to customers.
- PA helps in improving the channels of communication and interaction between employees and management.

Some Tools of the Trade for Performance Appraisal:

Given that performance appraisal offers multidimensional benefits, it would be beneficial to analyze what are the key tools for measuring performance in order to understand what really works and what doesn't. Organizations can change, adopt or adapt these tools depending on their individual preferences and competencies of their supervisors and managers.

At the outset it can be noted that performance appraisal frameworks can record, monitor and evaluate employee performance across 3 broad dimensions—trait based, behavior based, or results based (Baker et. al,1988). Performance appraisal methods and tools can be applied for gauging employee performance both at the individual level as well as the group level. Some of the popular tools of the trade are:

Graphic Rating Scales—It is the most widely used method for assessing trait based performance especially relating to personality, aptitudes, skills and abilities of employees. The criteria used for interpreting graphic rating scales leans more towards what is organizationally important for performance, rather than specific aspects related to the job. As a result graphic rating scales can form a common basis for interpreting performance of a large number of employees who are performing different categories of jobs. Rating scales vary from 1 to 5, each associated with interpretation such as low performance, average performance, good performance or excellent performance. The main advantage of graphic scales is that they are simple and easy to construct, can cover a wide array of jobs for assessing performance according to some predefined yardsticks. The disadvantage of graphic rating scales are that they have poor validity and reliability, create basis for subjectivity, and focus more on generic features associated with organizational performance rather than specific job related aspects.

Essay Method—It is widely used for rating employee performance using a descriptive framework of an essay, where performance is assessed under the generic categories such as overall impression about employee, performance capabilities of employees, knowledge, skills and abilities of employees, and general strengths and weaknesses of employees. The main advantage of the essay rating method is that it helps in providing a detailed and descriptive information regarding employee performance. Moreover it provides the supervisors with a greater degree of flexibility in analyzing and interpreting performance capabilities of employees in special areas that are overlooked in normal standardized objective formats for appraising performance. The main disadvantage associated with this method is that it is highly time consuming; analysis largely depends on writing skills and narration abilities of supervisors, and is prone to a higher degree of subjectivity than other objective formats for measuring performance. The Essay method is a useful tool but one that must be used in conjunction with other standardized objective formats.

Critical Incident Method—Critical incident technique is a useful tool for conducting behavior based performance appraisal of employees. Under this method, supervisors focus on recording certain critical behaviors of employees (positive or negative) as and when they unfold. The main advantage of critical incident technique is that performance of employees is measured not in a piecemeal fashion but on a continuous basis and focus is levied on monitoring critical behaviors as and when they happen. However the main disadvantage is that this method may result in overt supervision, may lead to creating excessive burden on supervisors and increase chances of errors in supervision as employees are to be evaluated on a continuous and frequent basis.

BARS Scale—Behaviorally Anchored Rating Scale (BARS) intends to overcome the shortcomings of the Graphic Rating scale by combining the tenets of critical incident technique with rating scales yardstick. BARS scale is a potent tool for measuring and evaluating behavior based performance of employees by identifying the key behavior of employees needed for their jobs. Identification of criteria of behaviors is made through close consultation between HR department and other concerned managers and supervisors for developing scales that can appropriately delineate behaviors in slots such as poor, average, good or excellent behavior. The main advantage of BARS method is that it is far more specific than other vague trait based methods and is predicated on the belief that desirable employee behaviors can lead to improved individual as well as collective organizational performance. However BARS also has a few disadvantages as developing criteria for required behaviors for specific aspects of job performance still remains a contested and subjective process. Utilization of BARS as a tool for employee performance is time consuming, costly and may result in creation of higher levels of stress in employees.

Management by Objectives (MBO)—It is a powerful tool for results based assessment of employee performance. Basically MBO method aims to create a clear framework of objectives and goals that the employees must accomplish for demonstrating performance. It needs to be noted that the goals given to employees for measuring and evaluating their performance must be SMART—specific, measurable, achievable, and realistic and within a specified time period (Locke & Latham, 2002). The main advantage of MBO performance appraisal is that it results in establishment of clear goals, performance standards and objectives and thereby helps in motivating employees for becoming more result oriented. However the process of establishment of goals is itself a subjective process, might sometimes take place unilaterally without employee involvement and may lead to creation of an obsessive result oriented atmosphere amongst employees.

360 Degrees Feedback/ Multisource Feedback—This has emerged quite recently as one of the predominant tools used by global organizations for improving learning or appraising performance of employees. Multisource feedback/ Multi-rater feedback method of performance appraisal differs from the conventional model of performance appraisal as instead of just relying on supervisors for appraising performance, feedback is sought from multiple sources such as supervisors, peers, subordinates, consumers, suppliers as well as from employees themselves(Denisi & Kluger,2000). The advantage of this method is that it helps in gaining a better overall picture about employees' performance collected from multiple perspectives. However it should be noted that 360 Degree method is more useful when it is used as a learning or improvement tool than as a performance appraisal tool. Secondly there are disadvantages associated with the anonymity of feedback as collection of data from multiple sources enhances the chances of information leaks. Moreover there is the associated problem of competence and knowledge of multiple raters in relation to the specific or contextual perspective of job performance of employees (Ghorpade, 2000). Last but not least 360 degrees feedback method turns out to be very expensive and time consuming method as it suffers from costly logistical bottlenecks in its administration, collection and analysis. Critics have even questioned the validity and effectiveness of the "self report dimension" associated with the 360 degree tool.

Forced Ranking (Forced Distribution Method)—This is a useful comparative evaluation tool for employee performance wherein raters rate employees according to a specified distribution curve. It is based on the primary assumption that the performance of employees conforms to a normal statistical distribution curve and the supervisors can rank employees across different points on the performance distribution curve depending on their quality of performance. For instance : 10 percent of employees can be ranked at the low level ; 20 percent below average; 40 percent average; 20 percent above average; and 10 percent can be ranked on the high level of the curve. While Forced distribution or ranking method can serve as a quick snapshot tool in ranking performance, nevertheless it can be noted that employee performance cannot always be represented in the form of a normal distribution curve. Moreover this method only assesses relative performance and might prove counterproductive in lowering employee's morale especially in cases where all employees have high ability and ranking of some employees as "poor performers" would lead to de-motivation of employees.

The above are some of the common tools for appraising and evaluating performance whether it is behavior based, traits based or results based.

It needs to be emphasized that performance appraisal is not a simple process but is a highly complex and challenging task. It is not just a simple matter of selecting a tool and progressing with evaluation of performance. PA would depend on the nature and type of performance criteria developed by the organization, the level of training and competencies that it's managers or supervisors have, the level of interaction that employees have in setting up of realistic objectives, the transparency and fairness associated with PA systems, and mechanisms of feedback that are in place for creating genuine growth and development of employees.

Beware of Some Common "Rater Errors" in appraising performance:

Outlining the tools of performance appraisal is one thing, knowing how to effectively use them in producing rational, unbiased evaluations is quite the other. It is commonly said that the effectiveness of a sword is determined not just by the quality of its blade but also by the prowess and valour of the person who wields the sword. In a similar vein, it can be stated that effectiveness of performance appraisal would not only be determined by the tools of the trade utilized for evaluating performance but also by the skills, training and competence of supervisors who are responsible for providing unbiased, and balanced judgments regarding employees' performance. Supervisors as humans are bound to commit mistakes; therefore they must be aware of some of the common rater errors that can cloud their judgment. Some of the well known rater errors that supervisors need to be aware of are:

- **Central Tendency**—a common mistake committed by supervisors when they erratically club the performance of employees around the average scale of performance. This is quite in keeping with the safe playing attitude of supervisors who might be apprehensive of reprisals or questioning from employees or unions.

- **Halo Error**—another common mistake of supervision wherein one aspect of employee's ability overshadows judgment of supervisors in other aspects of job performance. For instance if an employee is well behaved and submissive to supervisors, the good disciplinary aspect of employee behavior creates a halo effect for the supervisor who erroneously marks the employee undeservingly high on the productivity aspect of his job performance.

- **Spillover Effect**—this is another common mistake often committed by supervisors, wherein the past performance of an employee sways the present evaluation of an employee. For instance an employee may be an excellent performer in the past but at present he is failing to meet the standards of expectations, nevertheless he is provided with an inflated rating for present performance.

- **Similar to Me/ Ingroup vs Outgroup**—Supervisors also many times get swayed in their judgments by basing their decision on how similar the candidate is to the supervisor or what is the level of positive impression that the candidate has created on the supervisor. Furthermore in many instances supervisors feel that poor performance evaluation of employees may negatively reflect on them. In other instances employees may be unfavorably penalized if they are considered members of opposing group to the supervisor.

- **Primary & Recency Effects**: Supervisors judgments may get overtly swayed or clouded by employee behaviors during the beginning of the performance appraisal cycle or towards the end of the review period. This prevents development of balanced

71

appraisal or evaluation of employee across the entire period of performance review.

- **Personal Prejudices & Dispositions**—Supervisors are human beings. They are therefore not immune to misinterpreting performance of employees based on their inherent prejudices and stereotypes. Some raters are generically lenient and some supervisors may be unduly conservative in ranking employee performance.

It is clear from the above analysis that supervisors cannot be considered as infallible entities. They have their own share of weaknesses, biases and prejudices (Fletcher, 2001). Given the common traps that supervisors may fall victim to, it is necessary that supervisors should be regularly trained in the art of recording, monitoring, interpreting and evaluating performance.

Performance Appraisal: 7 vital steps for pulling it all together

Given that performance appraisal can be touted as a crucial process for gaining competitive advantage, motivating and inspiring employees, and improving overall organizational productivity, it can be strongly argued that companies must develop an integrated approach of performance appraisal in keeping with the strategic goals of the organization. Crucial questions that need to be answered in designing an effective performance appraisal system include aspects such as why the appraisal is important, what should be the key criteria for evaluating performance, who should be involved in the process, when and how should the appraisals take place?

The following are some of the useful generic steps that all organizations would find useful especially in designing, developing and implementing any performance appraisal framework:

1. **Create the Basis:** The first important step with performance appraisal is the identification of critical factors or criteria against which performance of employees need to measured. The basis for performance appraisal system needs to be systematically outlined in keeping with the knowledge, skills and abilities of workforce, the present framework of employee competencies and the intended future growth objectives of the organization and its employees.

2. **Collaboration & Consultation:** Development of criteria for assessing performance should not take place in a unilateral fashion but should be derived after several rounds of consultation with managers, supervisors, and employees. Often criteria developed in an isolated fashion without involvement of workforce results in setting up of unrealistic expectations.

3. **Focus on Processes & tools:** The next step is to focus on the broad processes that would be involved in conducting of performance appraisals. A decision must be made as to which aspects of appraisal are going to be assessed: should it be in the format of traits based assessment, behavior based assessment or results based assessment. Care should be taken to choose the tools of performance appraisal in view of the competencies of managers and supervisors who would be using, administering and interpreting these tools.

4. **Hire Knowledgeable Appraisers:** Given the crucial role of supervisors in conducting performance appraisal, it is essential for the company to choose knowledgeable supervisors who know the employee's job content and the context of the job and have requisite training in monitoring and evaluating performance.

5. **Educate, train & inform employees:** A crucial step on which the success of performance appraisal rests is educating employees and providing the right information about the rating formats that would be adopted. If performance appraisal is supposed to

influence employee's reward packages, contribute to decisions regarding employee promotions, transfers or terminations, then the employees have a right to be fully informed about the type and the fairness of the rating formats that are going to be used.

6. **Fairness & Transparency**—It is incumbent on the organization to adhere to the highest tenets of procedural and interpersonal justice in recording performance. It may be noted that employees would only accept performance appraisal systems as fair and just if they perceive that there is a high level of transparency and justice in the procedures carried out for evaluating performance. Employees must also perceive fairness in the way that they are treated by authority figures during the entire process of evaluating performance (Folger & Cropanzano, 1998).

7. **Sound System of Feedback**: Last but not least the final step for effective performance appraisal is to develop a sound framework of feedback. A performance appraisal system without a good feedback mechanism is like a body without its soul. Given that so much is at stake for employees, it is natural that employees need to be informed about what areas of deficiency were found in their performance, why were they not chosen for promotion, and how should they try to further improve themselves and their competencies? After all performance appraisal's main aim is to engender learning, growth and development of employees.

Useful Takeaways from Chapter

- Performance appraisal is one the core functions of HR.
- Performance appraisal is a multidimensional tool that records employee performance, helps motivate employees, and forms the foundation for future training.
- Performance appraisal can be defined as a process for identifying, observing, measuring and developing human performance.
- Performance can be appraised across many dimensions: traits based assessment, behavior based assessment and results based assessment.
- Performance appraisal holds benefits for all: Organization, managers and employees.
- Care should be taken in selecting the right tools for appraising performance.
- Supervisors should be aware of common "rater errors" and should be well trained.
- Key questions in appraising performance are: Why appraisal is to be conducted, what should be the criteria, who should be involved in the process, how and when should performance appraisal be conducted, and how can the system be made more transparent and fair?

CHAPTER 7

REWARDS & COMPENSATION

"Rewards & Compensation is like the gentle tap of encouragement on the shoulders of employees. It is a way for the organization to tell its employees—we care for you, and you matter for us".

Fawziya Al Araimi

Understanding the power of rewards & compensation is not just a necessity for the HR department, but it is an essential requirement for each and every department of the organization. Virtually every manager would agree that if the company is to gain competitive advantage, wants to motivate, attract and encourage employees and seeks to improve its productivity, then there is nothing more important than developing a sound system of rewards and compensation framework. The power of compensation for employees is well captured by the statement made by Jack Welch, the legendary CEO of General Electric—"*If you pick the right people and give them the opportunity to spread their wings and put **compensation** as a carrier behind it you almost don't have to manage them.*"

There is no denying the fact that compensation and reward mechanisms do seem to hold the key for organizational success and productivity in modern times. It is clear that if we are to look at employees as the most important assets of the organization, then we must pay greater attention to aspects of employee compensation that facilitates in not only attracting and retaining employees but also helps in motivating, encouraging and engaging employees for delivering best possible results (Fernie & Metcalf, 1999).

Anlayzing Reward Composition—A difficult and complex game:

Given that compensation & rewards are so important for employees it would be useful to understand what is the actual composition of the compensation systems. I would like to view the compensation systems or reward frameworks as a mixed potpourri that should include elements of both intrinsic and extrinsic rewards. When we talk of rewards we often erroneously equate rewards with only money. Rewards is something far more than money, it needs to cater not only to the extrinsic needs of employees such as pay, salaries, bonuses, commissions, fringe benefits etc., but also to the intrinsic needs of employees such as opportunities for growth, development, career advancement, challenging work, and greater responsibility(Baker et al, 1988).

Rewards is truly an amorphous entity, it can be materialistic, tangible, intangible, monetary, non monetary, financial, social, symbolic, externally administered or even self administered in the form of self recognition, self efficacy and self praise. Money makes the world "go round" can be seen as true in some capitalistic cultures, however it is not a universal statement for the broad diversity of organizations or employees out there on the global stage. Understanding the composition of reward structure does hold its own share of challenge, however the greater part of the challenge is associated with designing and delivering an effective reward and compensation framework for the organization, one that delivers results.

The greater challenge of designing compensation & reward systems

The problem with designing and delivering an effective compensation & rewards framework for employees seems to be exacerbated by the increasing chasm between the promise of theoretical frameworks and the challenges associated with objective reality of implementing and delivering results. The so called game of employee motivation, which is so central for any reward and compensation policy, is itself a highly complex task, which is much easier said than done. After all employee motivation cannot be seen as only an outcome of satiation of internal needs of employees but also has to take into account the cognitive, rational decision making processes that employees utilize to understand what makes them truly tick.

There are a multitude of factors one needs to consider in analyzing the design & effectiveness of rewards framework. Employees want to carefully understand how given rewards satiate their individual needs; intrinsic or extrinsic needs, how these rewards help to create congruence between their expectations and objective realities, how these rewards can be considered as commensurate to the gradient of inputs put in, how these rewards match up with perceived expectations of internal and external equity and finally how these rewards can help them condition, amplify or diminish their behavior?.

It becomes rather clear that while there is no denying of the importance associated with compensation frameworks, nevertheless these frameworks need to be seen as dynamic mechanisms, those that are in a state of constant evolution in keeping with the changing needs of the organization, employees and the business landscape in general.

Multiple Benefits of Reward & Compensation Frameworks:

Many managers often think that compensation or reward frameworks are beneficial only for the employees. This is completely an erroneous view, as compensation systems need to be seen as multidimensional systems that bestow benefits for the organization, management, consumers and of course the employees. The following briefly lists the benefits of a well defined compensation framework for any organization:

- A well designed compensation framework can act as a source of major competitive advantage.
- Compensation frameworks go a long way in improving the ability of the organization to attract, recruit, retain and engage employees.
- Nature of compensation systems prevalent in the organization can help in acting as a major source of motivation for the employees.
- Compensation systems can play a big role in boosting employee morale, organizational loyalty and employee job satisfaction.
- Attractive compensation systems can reduce costs due to employee turnover or absenteeism.
- Compensation systems can encourage peak performance and improve overall organizational productivity.
- Well designed systems can reduce friction with employees and lubricate better labor management relationships.
- Compensation systems help in building attractive brand image of companies as "employers of choice".
- Satisfied employees can create better standards for customer service and improve quality.
- Finally the nature of compensation system offered in companies does reflect in many ways the overarching philosophy of the organization in relation to management of employees.

5 Main Qualities for any Reward or Compensation Framework:

Given that compensation and reward frameworks shower multiple benefits, it is necessary to know what should be the five main qualities that any good compensation or reward framework must possess:

1. **Results Oriented:** The most important quality for any compensation framework is by far being result oriented. The whole idea behind rewarding employees or compensating them is to improve organizational performance and productivity. Therefore those compensation packages that don't work in eliciting "right type" of employee behaviors should be considered as failures.

2. **Competitive:** The second most important quality of any reward framework is that it must be competitive in the context of the business landscape where the organization operates. The main strategic intent of any compensation system is to attract, retain and motivate employees. If a compensation system is inward looking and operates without knowing what the competitive benchmarks are being offered by other firms, then achievement of results would surely become a distant dream.

3. **Motivational:** Another important quality for compensation frameworks is to serve as a motivational tool for bringing out the best potential of employees. In this regard compensation frameworks need to reflect a careful balance of options that can serve not only the extrinsic needs of employees but also their intrinsic needs.

4. **Equitable:** Equitability is probably the most important quality of a compensation system. Equitability should be achieved across two domains—internal equity—i.e equity in the way employees within the firm are being compensated and external equity—i.e the equity

between employees of similar organizations in a given business environment.

5. **Fair:** A related key quality for any compensation system is that it must be fair, information regarding the functioning of compensation systems should be distributed across employees in a clear and transparent manner. Both tenets of justice that is procedural justice and interpersonal justice should be strongly adhered to. A biased or prejudiced system of rewarding employees may increase crony culture but it will never enhance motivation across all folds of organizational workforce.

Crucial Questions regarding Compensation and Rewards:

Given the importance and multidimensional benefits that are associated with developing a sound compensation & reward framework, it is necessary for the organization to seek answers to some critical questions before designing their overall compensation philosophy. What needs to be emphasized is that the compensation philosophy of the organization should not be built in isolation but should be created in the light of the overall objectives of the company and the strategic choices that it makes.

Whether a company adopts a strategic position of cost leadership, differentiation or a focus, the compensation philosophy of the organization should be in close alignment with the overall organizational needs and objectives of the firm. There are some crucial questions that HR managers or even all managers from different departments need to answer for improving the competitiveness, efficacy and viability of their compensation systems. Some of these questions are:

What is our overall organizational mission and vision?.

What are the relevant compensation needs of our employees and how should we attempt to bridge the gap between expectations and reality?

> ➤ What are the specific areas in which we need to boost employee performance?
> ➤ How much can we pay employees without incurring losses?
> ➤ How can we make our compensation systems more competitive?
> ➤ How can our employees needs be satiated, internal and external needs?
> ➤ How does our compensation framework compare in relation to others?
> ➤ What kind of adjustment mechanisms need to be there for adjusting salaries to inflationary pressures?
> ➤ What kind of benefits should be given, why or why not?
> ➤ What should be the composition of our compensation packages—distribution between intrinsic or extrinsic rewards?
> ➤ How broad or specific should be the dispersion in compensation range across different grades or jobs?
> ➤ How can employee's perspective and participation be ensured?
> ➤ How should the channels of information be created for maintaining transparency in our compensation systems?
> ➤ How frequent should our pay raises be? How should pay raises be handled by special committees or individual managers?
> ➤ How often should our compensation frameworks be reviewed?

All these critical questions regarding compensation do help to highlight the magnitude of challenge and complexities that are involved in developing and designing effective systems of reward & compensation. One thing that becomes fairly evident from the discussion so far is that compensation systems and its associated philosophy should be seen as an evolutionary and dynamic system that has to adapt and adjust not just with the changing business landscapes but also with the changing needs of the organization and its employees.

Tools of the Trade for analyzing Compensation & Rewards:

Given the complexities associated with compensation system, it comes as no surprise that analyzing compensation & reward frameworks would pose a major challenge for managers. How compensation frameworks should be developed is a major decision that needs to be carried by HR department in close consultation and collaboration with line managers, supervisors and other department heads. Some of the useful tools used for analyzing employee compensation are presented below:

Job Analysis: This is a useful tool for deciding on compensation as well as for recruiting employees. Job analysis provides a systematic process for identification of key features of the job for creating the standards against which employee recruitment or compensation standards can be defined. It takes into account the job context, mental processes required, work output, information frameworks and the skills & competencies asked of employees. Job description & person specification are often the outcomes associated with job analysis. Interviews, Questionnaires and critical incident methods prove useful for job analysis.

Job Description/ Person Specification: Both of these tools can be used for both recruitment and compensation decisions. Job description highlights nature, content and scope of job; type of behaviors required, key responsibilities, functions and relevance of the jobs so that appropriate scale of compensation can be decided. In a similar way, person specification also helps to understand the profile of the candidate to decide what should be the compensation grade associated with him or her.

Job Evaluation: This is one of the most useful tools in making a systemic comparison of jobs for determining the appropriate levels of compensation based either on the job as a whole or the elements associated with the jobs. There are generally 4 main techniques:

a.) Ranking Method: Simplest method of evaluating jobs as a whole and arranging them from highest to lowest categories depending on either merit of the job or the relative difficulty level associated with performing the job. This ranking method can be used at the individual department level and then the findings can be collated at the organizational level to develop overall organizational rankings of jobs. However this method brings into play subjective factors and seems to be more suited for smaller organizations than larger organizations.

b.) Classification: This is a simple tool used for bunching jobs according to predetermined job classes or job grades such as Class 1 jobs, Class 2 etc. or Executive jobs, skilled workers, semi skilled workers etc. Advantage of this classification is that takes into account individual factors associated with the job and not the entire job as a whole, this method is easy to use and implement. However this method introduces some degree of subjectivity in bunching of jobs as mismatch may arise between job descriptions and grade descriptions. Moreover this method tends to overlook the individual differences between jobs that may exist even in the same classification of job.

c.) Factor Comparison Method—This is one of the most sophisticated tools for analyzing compensation. Jobs are not ranked as a whole in categories, but according to a series of factors such as mental effort, physical effort, skills levels, working conditions, problem solving abilities etc. Wage determination is based by differential weighing in of factors. While this method is most analytical, sophisticated and objective, nevertheless it is highly complex system that is extremely time consuming.

d.) Point Method: Similar to factor comparison method, though somewhat easier to design and implement. Jobs are expressed in terms of key factors and points are assigned to each of these factors according to a gradation scale of importance. Wage determination is based on adding up of the points and paying similar wages for jobs showing similar point totals. Factors generally looked for are skill level, responsibility, accountability, complexity of work, extent of effort required etc. Main advantage of this method is in its consideration of key factors as well as sub factors associated with the job. Disadvantage is the complexity and subjectivity that might result in determining the scale of importance of key factors for allocating points.

Salary Surveys/ Pay Structures: An age old proven method for developing the relevant benchmarks for salaries of employees. Salary surveys can be conducted by the HR department in close consultation with other departments of the organization so that perspective of employees and their expectations can be properly collected through interviews, and questionnaires. Salary surveys can also be conducted by utilizing the services of independent third parties or vendors to create a possible roadmap for guiding salary decisions. Relevant details of salary surveys should include average salary levels in the given sector, market or region, levels of inflation, kind of increments that employees want, minimum and maximum scales for different grade employees. Pay structures can also be similarly used that help in quantifying range of pay for different grades of employees.

9 Key Steps in Designing and Developing Modern Compensation Systems:

The following is a brief list of steps that can help in improving the effectiveness, viability and performance of any compensation framework for an organization. It is not necessary that all these steps need to be followed in the prescribed sequential format, but a good well balanced reward & compensation framework would be built utilizing many of the crucial elements outlined below:

1. **Be Aware of the Organizational Vision & Mission:** One of the first important step in developing a compensation framework is to be fully aware of the strategic choices that the organization has made, its overall organizational mission, vision and objectives. A reward and compensation framework needs to work in tandem and in the same direction as the overall organization mission and vision. After all the whole point behind compensation is to reward desirable employee behaviors and encourage peak performance. Both those objectives need to be in harmony with the strategic intent and the overarching organizational philosophy.

2. **Crafting a suitable Compensation Philosophy:** Being aware of organizational overarching goals and objectives is not enough. HR department in close consultation needs to develop a comprehensive compensation policy for the organization. In developing a holistic compensation philosophy we need to find answers to pertinent questions such as why is compensation required; what needs to be achieved, who is the compensation framework being devised for, what should be the composition of compensation framework, how should compensation policy be planned and implemented, etc.?

3. **Creating a Compensation Committee:** While a compensation philosophy can lay the conceptual

and theoretical ground work of how compensation frameworks need to be designed, nevertheless a formal compensation committee must be put in place to implement, administer and monitor the reward systems. The Compensation committee must be staffed by senior managers not only from HR but also from other departments and also have employee representatives so that a balanced framework of compensation is created. Decisions need to be taken whether compensation analysis should be handled internally or externally.

4. **Development of Objectives & Time Scale:** It is essential that the compensation frameworks to be put in motion need to have well defined objectives of what they are going to achieve as well as the manner in which this is going to be accomplished. Well formulated time scales should be developed with specified target dates that cover implementation, completion and review processes associated with compensation frameworks.

5. **Effective Utilization of Compensation Tools :** Once the objectives and time line for designing, implementing and monitoring of compensation frameworks is put in motion, then comes the requirement for effectively utilizing tools for analyzing compensation. Tools such as job analysis, job description can help in understanding not only the nature and content of the job but also about the specific requirements and responsibilities associated with the job. In addition main frame tools of job evaluation such as rankings, classification, factor analysis and point method can help in making comparative analysis of jobs for determining appropriate levels of compensation.

6. **Gradation Frameworks & Salary Structures:** Effective utilization and management of compensation tools would help in developing a good benchmark scale of job gradation as well as highlight a salary structure for these jobs. It is essential that the gradation

framework and salary structure should be formulated as objectively as possible, utilizing inputs from multiple sources such as HR managers, supervisors, department heads, and employee representatives in order to minimize subjective biases.

7. **Maintain Transparency in all documentation procedures:** Success of any compensation policy would largely rest on how transparent its compensation policies and frameworks are. It is essential therefore that all the documents relating to general company policy of compensation and rewards as well as the methodologies used should all be prepared in a clear and transparent manner. If employees doubt lack of fairness in compensation procedures then they are bound to get demotivated.

8. **Establish open channels of communication:** A major criteria that has to be followed in every procedure associated with designing reward frameworks is establishment of open channels of communication for dissemination of free and fair information. Effective compensation procedures warrant communication not in the unidirectional fashion that is from managers to employees but also from employees to management.

9. **Maintain Dynamism & Feedback:** Last but not least it is important that compensation frameworks should be treated not as static entities but as dynamic and evolutionary frameworks that need to be constantly monitored and reviewed. A crucial step therefore is to develop within compensation frameworks a sound system of feedback that can collect timely data from employees, managers and consumers.

Useful Takeaways from Chapter

- Reward & Compensation frameworks should provide a balanced mix of extrinsic and intrinsic rewards for employees.
- Rewards & Compensation frameworks shower multiple benefits for the organization, management, employees as well as consumers.
- Reward frameworks can help in gaining competitive advantage, boost employee motivation and improve overall organizational productivity.
- Compensation systems must be result oriented, competitive, equitable and fair.
- In developing a good compensation philosophy crucial questions need to be answered such as : what are the needs of the organization, what should the compensation system focus on, for whom the compensation is being designed, how competitive should it be, what should be the level of pay and frequency of increments, how should the system be designed, implemented, and reviewed?
- Some common tools for designing effective compensation frameworks are: Job Analysis, Job Description, Job Evaluation, and Salary Surveys & Pay Structures.
- Reward & Compensation frameworks need to be seen as dynamic and evolutionary systems that should proactively respond to competitive winds of change.

CHAPTER 8

HR & JOB DESIGN

"Domain of Job design or redesign focuses on the way by which tasks can be structured so that either people can fit to jobs or jobs can fit to people. It is all about increasing efficiency, productivity and performance."

Fawziya Al Araimi

The domain of designing of jobs is one of the most important processes for the overall performance and efficiency of the organization. It should not be seen as the sole responsibility of the HR department but as a fundamental design process that requires co-ordination, co-operation and collaboration of all departments. The centrality of the concept of jobs can be gauged from the fact that jobs are the basic unit that helps to define an employment relationship (Parker & Wall, 1998). When we join an organization we move into a system of contract with the management regarding what would be our job responsibilities, how should we discharge these responsibilities, what does the company expect from us, and what we can expect from the company?

In other words our joining an organization, working for an organization, receiving training from an organization, performing in an organization, getting rewards from an organization are all quite dependent on the jobs and the manner in which these jobs are designed.

If jobs are so central in whatever we do, it goes without saying that the processes related to the structuring or designing of the jobs, tasks, roles and responsibilities should be considered equally important not only for employees but also for the organization as a whole.

Benefits of Job Design: Employees, Management, Consumers—

Job design offers multiple benefits for all stakeholders of the organization; employees, investors and consumers. Through development of good job designing frameworks, employees can become more motivated and satisfied to perform, organization can improve its performance, output and efficiency, consumers can benefit by receiving higher quality end products and pleasure of dealing with motivated, efficient and responsive employees. The following is a brief list of numerous benefits that good job design frameworks can offer:

- Job Design can improve overall organizational performance and efficiency.
- Job Design can improve motivation levels of employees and enhance their job satisfaction.
- Job Design can improve employee morale and work life balance for employees.
- Job Design can reduce costs for the company due to employee turnover and absenteeism.
- Job design can facilitate in generating higher profits for the company, thus improving the bottom line.
- Consumers can benefit from improved quality, dependability and efficiency associated with product offerings and service deliveries.

HR : A key player in Job Design :

It becomes quite evident from the discussion so far that Job Design is a multidimensional process that offers a myriad range of benefits for all aspects of the organization and therefore needs collaborative effort and involvement from all departments of the organization. While I agree that all departments and managers have a role to play in the process of job designing, nevertheless the involvement of HR professionals is most warranted because their role is quite central in the whole process of job design. HR is a strategic business partner for the organization; therefore its involvement is warranted in any process that improves organizational performance, efficiency and productivity.

- HR professionals need to be involved as they are employee champions and jobs are the central part of any employment relationship.
- HR professionals are entrusted with motivating, empowering and improving the human capital pool. Job design processes relate to all these three facets.
- HR plays a leading role in key processes of employee recruitment and selection, training, performance appraisal etc. Hence HR professionals must have a thorough understanding of how jobs are structured or designed.
- HR professionals also develop frameworks of compensation; job design helps to create the very standards against which employees are to be monitored.
- Knowledge of job design is essential for conducting all sub processes such as job analysis, person description/ specification, job evaluation etc.

4 Main Objectives of Job Designing:

So far the chapter has revolved around how important job designing is for all stakeholders of the organization and how HR should assume a leadership role in the process of job designing. At this stage it would be useful to highlight what are the 4 key objectives associated with the process of job design:

Efficiency: Quite simply put it can be noted that efficiency in organizational processes is the chief objective behind any framework of job design or redesign. After all well structured job design frameworks can improve quality of processes by removing errors; enhance the speed with which these processes are completed and reduce costs through optimal utilization of resources.

Effectiveness: The second major objective happens to be improving the effectiveness of work processes. Job design helps in improving the dependability of processes, creates greater flexibility in the way tasks are structured and improves the quantity and quality of output produced.

Competitiveness: It does not take a degree in rocket science to understand that if processes become streamlined to be more efficient, effective and productive, if employees experience higher levels of motivation and satisfaction then the firms can hope to gain and sustain the much needed competitive edge over their competitors.

Safety & Balance: Another major objective of job design process is to create better standards of safety in work practices. Well designed frameworks are based on sound principles of ergonomics that focuses on making procedures of working more comfortable and efficient. Furthermore job design principles can facilitate in achieving better work life balance for employees and significantly improve their quality of working life.

Job Design or Redesign: Is there a difference?

Given the importance of job design frameworks for modern organizations and the wide ranging benefits that it can provide, it is sometimes erroneously thought that the concept of Job design is something unique or recent(Campion et. al, 2005). However this in not the case as the origins of paradigm of job design can be traced back to the advent of industrial revolution. During the early 1900s principles of scientific management served as the guiding cornerstone for creating frameworks of job design. The mechanistic approach to job design was the norm of the day whose central tenets revolved around principles of centralization, task specialization, standardization and simplification of work practices for increasing productivity and worker efficiency (Wall & Martin, 1994). Job designing was based on Tayloristic principles of scientific management that assumed that workers were inherently lazy and therefore managers needed to closely control, monitor and supervise employees. Jobs could be divided into tasks, tasks could be subdivided into basic movements and through conducting of time and motion studies; it was possible to develop one best of doing things (Parker et.al, 2001). The focus seemed to be levied on making employees fit to their jobs, rather than making jobs fit to people.

However it was soon noted that while standardization, rationalization and deskilling of jobs helped in improving organizational performance, nevertheless these resulted in lower levels of employee motivation, exacerbated employee morale and reduced employee job satisfaction.

With the increasing importance of centrality of employees for the organization, it was soon felt that levels of employee motivation, satisfaction and morale are important, therefore jobs needed to be redesigned through infusion of principles of job enrichment and motivation (Wall & Martin, 1994). Herzberg through his famous two factor theory model had already demonstrated that for employee motivation intrinsic factors such as challenging work, achievement, responsibility, and career advancement opportunities were more relevant than extrinsic factors such as working conditions, salary, job security etc (Storey, 2001).

The need for improving employee motivation and satisfaction created a strategic shift away from principles of job design to the new arena of job redesigning that was intent on making jobs more intrinsically rewarding for employees through vertical loading(up skilling) of jobs and enhancing of responsibility, challenge, autonomy and feedback associated with jobs. The new emphasis therefore seemed to be focused more on making jobs fit to employees rather than making employees fit to their jobs as was the case with the initial frameworks of job design.

Under this new genre of Job Redesigning, it can be noted that the Job Characteristics model propounded by Hackman & Odham (1976) can be considered as a gold standard or a major watershed in the arena of Job redesigning. The simple assertion of this model was that if the goal was to improve employee satisfaction, employee motivation and organizational performance then the core characteristics of jobs such as skills variety, task identify, task significance, autonomy and feedback needed to be improved. According to Hackman & Oldham (1976) the 5 core characteristics that hold the key for improving the overall motivating potential score (MPS) associated with jobs were:

- **Skill variety**: doing different things, using varied skills and abilities
- **Task identity**: doing a complete task from beginning to end
- **Task significance**: the meaningful impact the job has on others
- **Autonomy**: discretion to do the job as one sees fit.
- **Feedback**: clear, regular and timely information about outcomes or performance can come from the work itself or from other people

From the discussion it can be deduced that there is a considerable distinction between the concepts of job design and redesign. While Job design through its principles of work standardization, rationalization and simplification focused on improving only organizational productivity, job redesign through vertical enrichment of jobs, upskilling, enhanced autonomy, and feedback created higher level of employee motivation, empowerment and satisfaction. The central focus of job design is to make employees fit to the requirements of jobs, whereas the central focus of job redesign is to make jobs fit to needs and requirements of employees. Though generically job design can be seen as an all encompassing paradigm which includes within its fold both the processes of job design as well as job redesign. The choice of specific frameworks would depend largely on the overall organizational objectives, the type of technological frameworks used, and the kind of operations that the organizations are engaged in.

7 Vital Steps for developing good frameworks of Job Design :

It can be mentioned at the outset that job designing is a complex and challenging process that needs to be developed by HR department in close consultation and collaboration with other managers and departments. The following is a brief list of practical steps that managers can undertake:

1. **Be Aware of the Organizational Needs & Objectives**: The first requirement is to be thoroughly aware of what are the needs and objectives of the organization. This is essential as it helps in developing the roadmap for developing, implementing and institutionalizing the principles of job design.
2. **Awareness about Technological frameworks**: The second important step is to be aware about the type of technological frameworks that the organization has. This is highly relevant because it reveals information about the present level of knowledge, skills and competence of workforce and what frameworks are

needed for simplification or enrichment of jobs and tasks as the case may be.

3. **Focus on the nature of activity of the organization:** Analysis of nature of activity of the organization is crucial because based on it, decisions regarding choice of job design or redesign frameworks can be taken. If the organization is a factory unit or is a fast food restaurant then focus can be levied on standardization of tasks as highlighted by core principles of mechanistic model of job design. If organization is engaged in consulting, banking or other activities then principles of job redesign are more appropriate through levying of focus on vertical enrichment of jobs.

4. **Focus on the type and the level of the job:** While general nature of activity of the firm helps to outline the broad canopy framework of job design, focus needs to be narrowed down to the specific content, nature and scope of the job. Additionally consideration must be given to the level of job; that is analysis needs to be made whether the job offering is at the worker level, supervisor level or managerial level.

5. **Collect Information through a collaborative approach:** Managers need to effectively use tools such as Job Analysis, Position analysis, job description or person specification. This information should be developed not in isolation by HR but through an interactive and collaborative approach with other departments. Utilization of tools such as Job Diagnostic surveys, critical incident methods and interviews can help in unraveling vital information about requirements of jobs as well as the needs and expectations of the employees.

6. **Focus on improving the Motivating Potential Score (MPS) :** An essential part of job design process is analyzing how jobs can be made more challenging, satisfactory and motivational for employees. In

this regard managers need to analyze how they can improve core characteristics of jobs such as skill variety, task identity, and task significance. Also to empower employees managers need to give them greater autonomy in decision making and provide constructive feedback channels for making workers aware of their work results. After all in modern organizations there is a persistent trend to move towards flatter hierarchical structures where workers have to be given greater freedom and autonomy for facilitating their genuine participation.

7. **Regularly review and monitor:** Given the dynamism associated with modern day jobs and technologies, it is essential for HR professionals to constantly monitor and review their present frameworks of job design to identify the areas where positive changes can be incorporated. It is necessary to keep an open mind, collect regular feedback from employees and managers regarding how jobs can be further improved in light of the expectations of the management as well as of the employees.

Some important challenges associated with Job Design:

While there are myriad benefits associated with job designing, nevertheless there are some significant challenges also associated with this complicated process:

- HR practitioners have to be careful in designing which model of job design is most appropriate for their organisation; a careful analysis of objectives of organisations must be made as different frameworks of job design may lead to different outcomes (Campion et. al, 2005).
- HR practitioners also need to understand how tradeoffs can be carefully balanced between organisational

productivity and levels of employee motivation and satisfaction in view of the needs of the organisation.

- HR professionals have to weigh in the challenges posed by their organisation's technological constraints. Technological systems on one hand have led to deskilling of jobs through absorption of traditional skills; on the other hand have created a greater demand for higher cognitive and technical skills in employees.

- HR practitioners also have to confront the constraints posed by their type of personnel system frameworks. Job design needs to be in sync with the overall HR philosophy of the organisation.

- HR practitioners need to prepare careful diagnostics regarding the nature of work, the content and scope of the job so that the motivation level score of jobs can be improved.

- HR practitioners need to prevent any major gaps between expectations of management and expectations of employees.

- Last but not least HR practitioners face the challenge of deciding what should be the appropriate unit for conducting job design; should it be at the level of the job, or at the level of duties, or should it be at the level of the tasks associated with the job?

Useful Takeaways from Chapter

- Job designing or redesigning is all about improving design of work practices by either fitting employees to jobs or fitting jobs to employees.
- Job design offers multiple benefits; improves organizational performance, and employee motivation and satisfaction.
- Job design requires consultation and collaboration between all major departments of organization.
- HR can assume the lead in process of job designing because HR professionals as employee champions are responsible for improving employee motivation.
- The 4 major objectives of any job design process are: efficiency, effectiveness, competitiveness and work safety.
- HR professionals in conducting job design must bridge the expectations gap between employees & management.

CHAPTER 9

HR & CHANGE MANAGEMENT

"Change is like a moving platform that helps the organizations to learn and grow. If you have the courage to manage the winds of change then you can climb the highest peaks of excellence and swim across the deepest ocean of challenges."

Fawziya Al Araimi

It has been often said "the only thing that is constant in this world is change". In modern times the relevance of this aphorism has become all the more important. We live in a dynamic world where adoption, adaptation and embracing of change has become the norm of the day. Whether we think of ourselves as individuals or as representatives of organizations, successful handling of change has emerged as a quintessential necessity (Kotter, 1996). Many managers mistakenly believe that change is needed only when organizations want to move forward, they fail to realize that change is needed not just for progression but even for retaining or holding on to what the organizations already have. Change is thus a framework that defines the very survival and existence of modern day organizations.

Organizations don't make people; people make organizations and give it identity. So success and survival of organizations depends on how effectively companies practice the art of people management. The concept of people management is quite closely identified with the ability of organizations for handling change, infusing competencies and capacities for handling change, and institutionalizing change in the organization's cultural fabric.

Barger & Kirby (1995) believe that change unfolds across 4 major dimensions; strategy, structure, technology and people. The central focus however has to be levied on the "people dimension" of change as all the other dimensions are inherently dependent on, or are merely subservient to the way employees or people in the companies understand, handle and embrace the winds of change. Given the centrality of people in organizations, change has become an ever present feature of modern organizational life.

Benefits of Effective Change Management:

Forces of globalization, liberalization, ushering in of new technological frameworks, rapidly changing socio-political and economic conditions have all made modern companies become highly sensitive to the forces of change. Change can be visualized as a multidimensional and multifaceted process that provides benefits for all stakeholders; the consumers, the employees and the investors. Some of the major benefits of effective change management are outlined below:

- Effective change management strategies can help firms gain competitive advantage.
- Change management can help improve organizational performance & productivity.
- Change management may lead to greater efficiency through optimal and cost effective utilization of resources.
- Effective change management allows better adoption of latest technological frameworks.
- Change management can help firms become more viable and sustainable in future.

- Well managed change can help consumers by providing higher quality services and provide them with greater choice.
- Company's dexterity in handling levers of change, would determine how successful the company is in people management, managing resistance to change and creating higher motivation and commitment in its employees.

It becomes evident that no facet of the organization is immune to, or isolated from the winds of change. Change touches every aspect of the organization; therefore the urgent need is for the companies to be in a state of constant preparedness for handling this ever present feature of organizational life.

Role of HR in Management of Change:

It is clear that developing the capacity to change and adopting proactively the forces of change is essential for virtually every department of the organization—be it sales, marketing, production, finance or even HR. Whichever perspective we adopt—be it the consumers, investors, or the employees, no one can trivialize the power and potency of the forces of change and the need for the organization to submit to these forces. If change is such an omnipresent entity in organizational life, then the key question that arises is who should lead, manage, implement or institutionalize change?

While every department would like to put forward their unique credentials for managing change, I feel that it is the HR department that must play a leading role in the practice of managing change. From my perspective, I feel that HR professionals should see themselves as occupying the mantle of leadership in managing change; they need to visualize themselves as explorers and identifiers of change, analyzers for understanding the impact of change, and planners and implementers of change in the overall organizational framework. While HR can assume a leadership role in management of change, nevertheless the entire process of change is one that requires careful balance, co-ordination and collaboration between multiple departments and different layers of organizational hierarchy (Kanter et. al,1992).

We must not forget that HR is all about people management. People (employees) are always central to any facet of change, as success of any type of change across any dimension would ultimately hinge on the ability of the organization to involve and engage its employees. HR as so called employee champions can act as key agents for sponsoring change by developing the shared need, promoting communication, participation and involvement of workforce, and facilitate in reducing resistance in employees to change due to their perceptual, emotional and cognitive blocks. Moreover HR has a stellar role to play in institutionalizing of change into the core cultural fabric of the organization for instilling change in the core values, beliefs and assumptions of an organization's employees.

The following is a brief list of reasons why HR should assume leadership role in management of change:

- HR is a strategic business partner; effective change management is good for organizational performance, productivity and sustainability.
- HR professionals as employee champions are most adept in handling the central "people" dimension of change.
- HR professionals can tackle effectively with employee resistance as they have expertise in tackling personnel issues.
- HR helps in creating a shared need, in promoting participation and communication and in mobilizing employee commitment for change.

- HR helps in developing the capacity and competencies for handling change by training and rewarding employees.
- HR professionals as job designers can contribute to change by building new systems, structures, and processes for ensuring optimal fit of jobs to people.
- HR professionals can also play a major role in institutionalizing and embedding of change in the core cultural values, beliefs and assumptions of the organization.

Understanding the Meaning of Change:

I find that Change can often be likened to a multicoloured prism that creates new meaning of change depending on the perspective of the person who gazes through it. For instance if a sales professional were to gaze through this magical prism, change for him, would denote the changing preferences, attitudes and dispositions of consumers that the organisation must address. On the other hand if a production professional were to gaze through this magical prism, change would denote new frameworks of technology that need to be adopted to streamline production capabilities and improve employee productivity. In short the very meaning of change means different things to different people.

But the important question that often emerges is, while there may be discrepancy attached in interpreting the meaning of change, is there at least some unanimity in relation to the general definition of change? The answer however is not encouraging as there are myriad definitions associated with this dynamic entity called change.

Different scholars have put forth their divergent interpretations regarding the content, nature or the very scope associated with change. For some scholars change can be seen as a linear movement from one point to another point, however for others, change can be seen as a gradual, continuous and evolving process that cannot have a predefined beginning or an end (Bamford & Forrester, 2003). In a similar vein there is considerable divergence associated with how we define the process of change management.

From one perspective organisational change management can broadly defined as the process of continually reviewing organisation's structure, direction, strategies and capabilities in order to satiate the needs of internal and external customers. On the other hand from the other perspective, change management can be seen as an amalgamation of strategic, structural and systemic changes initiated in order to move an organisation from current state or organisational and sociological setting to a new state of organisational and sociological setting (Storey, 2001).

What ever be the ambiguity or confusion associated with change or for that matter the process of change management, one thing is quite certain that change has become an ever present feature of our modern organisational life.

We can love it, hate it, embrace it or mould it, but we cannot just overlook it. Process of change has become one of the major defining characteristics of our very existence in the context of modern industrial civilization.

Different types of Change: Change a many splendoured thing :

I would like to visualize change, just as if it were flowing water, it is incumbent on us, how we harness the power and potency of this water; we can plan ways to harness its force of energy or we can brace ourselves to be swept away by a transformational force such as that of a tsunami. It is interesting to note that there is no one best way of managing change, as change itself is a multi splendored entity that comes in different shapes and sizes. Part of the enigma associated with change is due to the inherent dynamism that is associated with change, as it can never be straight jacketed into one format.

One needs to be constantly agile, one needs to be always on one's tip toes in order to manage and harness the forces associated with different types and forms of change. What seems fundamental for every manager is that they should have an in depth knowledge about the different types of change so that they can have some sort of a route map in tackling the process of change. The following framework lists out some common types of change that managers need to be aware of:

- **Gradual vs Punctuated:** Change can be seen as a cumulative, gradual or evolving process or it can be seen as a punctuated process. Gradual processes may belong to the genre of incremental changes or first order change—one step at a time, and punctuated model of change accommodates both incremental and radical forces of change. Change in the punctuated format shows periods of stationery equilibrium where incremental changes take place, as well short periods of marked discontinuity where transformational or radical changes can take place(Allen, 1985).
- **Developmental, Transitional, Transformational:** Developmental changes are similar to first order or incremental changes that often focus on rectifying specific aspects of an organization. Transitional change focuses on moving the organization from present state to desirable state through utilizing second order or radical changes. Transformational changes are always spectacular and radical in nature that inherently focus orchestrating substantial changes in strategy, structure, systems and culture of the organization.
- **Planned Vs. Emergent Change:** Planned change can be visualised as moving from one state to another through pursuit of chronologically defined sequential steps. Planned change can be seen as a linear, sequential

and rational process that is a product of conscious reasoning and action. Emergent change visualizes change as an emergent process that may arise due to external or internal factors beyond managerial control, is non linear, non sequential and an irrational process. Emergent change emphasizes that change needs to be seen as an open ended, unplanned process that cannot have predetermined beginning or end points (Allen, 1985).

- **Episodic vs. Continuous:** Episodic change can be seen as something that is infrequent, intentional and discontinuous; often would involve radical or second order changes (Weick & Quinn, 1999). Continuous change on the other hand visualizes change as incremental or first order in nature as an ongoing, evolving and cumulative process.
- **Top Down Vs. Bottom up:** There is also discrepancy in classification of change depending on the direction in which change unfolds. Top down change is often seen as being operated from the top towards the bottom or manager led change. On the other hand the bottom up change is more reflective of an emergent change, where change rises from the bottom to the top and cannot be closely monitored.

A generic prescriptive framework for managing change: 10 Broad Steps in Management of Change

It becomes quite clear that change comes in different forms, shapes and sizes. Knowledge about the type of change, scale and direction of change can provide the managers with the much needed route map of how change needs to orchestrated, tackled, planned for or even implemented and institutionalized. Having the broad outline of a possible route map is one thing, developing or planning the practical frameworks necessitated for managing change is quite the other.

It may be recalled that HR managers in consultation with the other senior department heads can act as eyes and ears of the organization in handling the processes of change. It needs to be noted that there is no one specific framework by which change can be effectively managed as different scholars have forwarded different recipes for handling change (Kotter, 1996; Kanter et.al,1992). The following is a generic framework, based on different models of change management that managers can employ as a useful general guide for managing the winds of change.

1. **Understand the Need for Change:** The first step for managers is to keep an open mind and understand the need for change. Managers should investigate where the change needs to take place across which dimension—strategy, structure, systems, technology or people. Investigate why is the change necessary, what are the forces aiding change and what could be the possible forces preventing change. Sense of alertness, openness and dexterity in understanding the need for change and reacting to it helps to define the fundamental criteria of success for managing change.

2. **Identify the type of change:** It is essential for managers to understand what is the type or nature of change that is required in the organization. Identification of the type of change can help the managers outline a rough sketch or a route map of how change would unfold and how it can be dealt with or harnessed. Some key questions in this regard that need to be answered are: Is the kind of change needed developmental in nature, or is it transitional or should it be seen as transformational? Can the change be tackled in a planned manner or is it of the emergent type? Should change be infiltrated on a continuous basis or should it be handled through specific transformational shifts?

3. **Identification of Sponsors of Change:** Once the need and type of change have been ascertained,

it is incumbent on organizations to create a quick framework as to who would lead or sponsor the change process. Allocation of responsibility for heading or leading the change or even reacting to and absorbing change is a key step in successful management of change. This is much simpler in case of planned changes, but even in case of emergent changes, we need to bring in some form of cemetery and order in management of change so that change process is not allowed to run like a headless chicken. Do not allow change to behave like a rudderless ship, unguided ships rarely reach shore.

4. **Create a sense of shared need:** Change is a multidimensional process that can benefit multiple stake holders. It needs to be handled through collaboration and co-operation. It is essential therefore to create a sense of shared need. Managers must understand why the change is required, employees must relate to the value and importance of change, investors should be apprised about the benefits of change, all perspectives need to be taken into consideration. A collaborative change framework that brings everyone on board increases dramatically the chances of success.

5. **Shape a balanced vision:** Vision is far more than painting a rosy picture of what should be the ideal position, it is something that needs to be practical, tangible and achievable. Vision needs to be created through an interactive and collaborative framework where involvement should be sought from multiple stakeholders. Do not just impose a vision on others, it would surely fail. Managers must know where the organization wants to be after change, employees must realize what behavioral modifications they need to bring about, investors must realize how these changes can benefit the organizational interests and those of the consumers. Vision must also resonate a feeling of realism laced with practicality. It should be realistic

and not just a dream in the specific context of the competencies and the capacity of the organization.

6. **Open bidirectional channels of communication:** Effective communication is probably the most important process for successful management of change. The vision cannot just sit prettily on the company publication reports, it needs to be translated and communicated across the organizational hierarchy. Managers must know what to do, employees must realize what should be done, and management must listen to what employees have to say in developing frameworks of co-operation and mutual commitment. Communication should not be in the form of a "unilateral command" system flowing from top to bottom, but should be in the form of a bidirectional flexible format that readily incorporates the relevant suggestions from employees' perspective also. Good, transparent communication also tackles effectively resistance of employees. One cannot overlook the fact that every form of change would essentially result in disrupting of present status quo, employees have a natural propensity of resisting to change. Management therefore must look at change from perspective of employees and devise ways for effectively transforming their resistance to change into acceptance of change by outlining what are the intended benefits that change would bring for the organization as well as organization's employees.

7. **Build capacity and develop competencies:** Communication alone is powerless, unless and until it is backed up by credible investments in building of capacity and competencies. For every kind of change to be embraced or institutionalized an organization needs to build the relevant capacity for adopting or adapting to change. Employees have to be provided with new competencies; knowledge, skills and abilities, they need to be infused with new levels of motivation so that change percolates quickly and

efficiently across the organization. Building of capacity and competencies brings about a greater sense of participation, empowerment and involvement of employees in the overall process of management of change.

8. **Line up multiple goal posts:** Often the greatest difficulty with change is that one idealized goal is given and everything else is forgotten. This is similar to showing the employees the peak of a distant mountain, without outlining a possible route map that teaches them how to reach there. It is important therefore to break the ultimate goal into multiples of small realistic goal posts. After all one cannot just fly to the top of a mountain without taking the very first step. Breaking down of the bigger goal into smaller manageable goal posts can serve as a guide for both employees and managers in helping them move forward, one step at a time. Every small goal post that is achieved would bring with it a new sense of euphoria and excitement in workforce that a step in the right direction has been achieved.

9. **Don't let the tempo slag:** Successful change management is all about the involvement of the mind, soul and the body. Multiple goal posts would lead to a sense of motivation and excitement that needs to be further built upon and consolidated for change to be successful. While every change cannot be sequentially planned, but management can ensure that once the tempo for change has been built, the organizational cart should not come to a standstill again. It always takes a massive effort to build a momentum, therefore organizations need to capitalize on it as much and as fast as they can.

10. **Make the Changes Last:** The ultimate step is to make these changes stick to the cultural fabric of the organization. If change has to be institutionalized, then it must percolate to the core cultural beliefs, values and assumptions of the organization. Schein (1985) from

the anatomical perspective argues that organizational culture is made up of three layers, the most visible outer layer of artifacts or outward manifestations, the middle layer of espoused values and the deepest layer of core beliefs, values and attitudes. For the change to stick, it must penetrate to the inner most layer of organizational core values, beliefs and assumptions. Organizations also must create regular frameworks for reviewing and evaluating change in order to ensure that it gets properly absorbed in the organization.

Leading Problems in Management of Change:

While change management has emerged as an indispensable entity for modern organization, nevertheless it can be noted that the rate of failure of change management initiatives is fairly high. On an average it is predicted that as many as 7 out 10 initiatives of change end up as dismal failures. The following is a brief list of some of the major causes that can be associated with failure of change initiatives. It would be useful for managers to avoid these common mistakes so that the forces of change can be efficiently harnessed:

- **Poor Organisational Diagnostics**—Managers often fail to conduct proper organisational diagnostics as a result they remain unaware of the urgent need and requirement of change or the manner in which the change should unfold. Moreover managers remain ignorant about the type of change that is needed, be it developmental, transitional or transformational. Ignorance might provide temporary bliss but such state of bliss cannot exist in the rapidly evolving business landscape of modern organisations.
- **Inability of creating a sense of shared need:** Another top reason behind change failure is the inability of management to create a framework of shared need for management of change. Change does not take

place in a vacuum; it needs to take place through collaboration and participation of all the stakeholders who would be affected by the process of change. Unless and until everyone is onboard and know how change would affect them, a comprehensive all encompassing support for change cannot be properly manifested.

- **Too Big a Picture:** Most change initiatives fail because they start with too utopic or too unrealistic vision frameworks. Wisdom dictates that while painting a rosy picture about vision is good, but unless and until it is realistically achievable it can prove counterproductive. Vision must have the capability of being translated into palpable reality.

- **Poor Communication:** Weak communication is probably one of the most important reasons behind failed change initiatives. Process of change always depends on clarity and effectiveness of communication. Managers must know what they are supposed to do, line supervisors must know what kind of motivation is needed to be created in employees, employees must realise what are the organisational expectations from them and what kind of behaviours they have to demonstrate.

- **Too Top Down or Insular:** Change often fails because managers tend to adopt or advocate for an overtly top down approach to change. They mistakenly believe that all facets of change can be calculated in a linear, sequential or rational fashion often ignoring the inherent dynamism and unpredictability that is associated with change. By adopting a top down approach managers often advocate blinkers on approach for managing change without realising the multidimensional influences that change initiatives are generally subject to.

- **Overlooking the Human Dimension:** Overlooking of human dimension which is the central element in any change process is probably the most important reason behind failure of all change initiatives. Managers often fail to realise that change ultimately has to be implemented and institutionalised with the help of employees. Therefore unless employee resistance is curbed, employees' competencies and capacity for handling change are created and employees' genuine participation is solicited, none of the intended objectives of successful change management can be realised.

- **Piecemeal Approach:** Companies fail to realise that change should be seen as a continuous and an ongoing process not as a temporary flash in the pan. By focussing on a piecemeal approach minor changes or superficial changes can be instituted and not the fundamental changes that are needed for successful organisational transformation. Management must develop a comprehensive approach for monitoring and evaluating change on a continuous basis if they want to capitalise on the positive benefits associated with change.

- **Poor Cultural infusion:** Change mostly fails because many a times change processes fail to penetrate the core cultural layers of the organisation. For change to be properly institutionalised, it is essential that change processes and implementation of change frameworks should penetrate the core values, beliefs and assumptions that define an organisation and its employees.

- **Lack of Leadership Involvement:** For change to be successful leadership must be holistically involved in the process of management of change. Involvement of leadership is required not only at the strategic level but also at the operational level to create the sense of motivation and involvement in workforce to adapt and embrace proactively the winds of change. Leadership's personal involvement in the process of change through strategy development, role modelling, coaching and mentoring can help in transmitting the right signals to managers and employees of the organisation that the top management is serious about change.

Useful Takeaways from Chapter

- Effective change management helps in improving organizational performance, gaining competitive advantage and ensuring profitability.
- Change management can be beneficial for all stakeholders; investors, consumers and employees.
- Change takes place across different dimensions. People dimension is the most important dimension.
- HR professionals have a leading role to play in management of change as they are the employee champions and personnel specialists.
- There is no simple definition of change as it comes in different shapes and sizes.
- Managers should develop a general framework for management of change and adapt it depending on the nature or type of change they need to manage.
- Managers would do well to avoid some of the common errors in management of change such as: poor organizational diagnostics, lack of shared need, overoptimistic vision, poor communication, overlooking of human dimension, and handling of change in a piecemeal, isolated or in a unilateral fashion.

CHAPTER 10

HR & WORK LIFE BALANCE

"Happiness in life can be seen in the form of an equation; Happiness = Work Satisfaction + Life Satisfaction. We often forget that work and life are integrally related and satisfaction in one at the cost of the other is simply not worth the effort."

Fawziya Al Araimi

All work and no play makes Jack a dull boy. Ironically this pithy axiom holds significant relevance even in context of modern organizations. Work without balance in components of life such as family, community and self is like a body with no soul, a ship without a rudder, a life without happiness. Many religious texts and treatises often espouse that true satisfaction in life only results from gaining happiness across the multiple dimensions of life; personal, professional, social, and moral. Work life balance in this light seems to be a step in the right direction that modern companies hope to achieve.

It has often been remarked that our very existence, identity and our personality is largely impacted by the satisfaction that we derive from domains of personal and professional life. These need to be in harmony, finely balanced for satiating our needs and achieving true satisfaction. Forces of globalization, ushering in of new technological revolutions, intensification of work, and increasing competition have all resulted in creating a highly stressful environment for employees, where our work problems have often permeated into our personal lives. As a result organizations on their part must strive to provide their employees with initiatives that can help achieve better balance in their personal and professional domains. In the industrial era it was quite erroneously believed that work and life could be seen as two separate, unconnected domains as if to say in Mark Twain's words that east is east, and west is west, and "never the twain shall meet". However reality is quite far from it, not only have east and west come closer to each other in many ways, but also the modern companies have increasingly realized that work and life need to be seen as an intricately linked, symbiotically connected and mutually beneficial domains.

It follows then if the companies want to improve their overall performance, emerge as an employer of choice, gain competitive advantage though improved levels of employee motivation and commitment, reduce employee turnover, they must undertake creation of well planned work life balance initiatives and programs.

Defining Work Life Balance

Quite simply put "work life" balance can be seen as the reconciliation between paid work and life, or the balance that needs to be orchestrated between work and non work demands. However hidden in this very definition is a reflection of the myriad challenges faced, as both work and life are highly complex and multifaceted domains that cannot be exactly quantified or outlined. Work also includes components that are not necessarily paid for, and life includes multiple influences from family, self, community and society (Hyman & Summers, 2004). Nevertheless challenges in conceptual and definitional domains should not be treated as a convenient excuse by the companies for extricating themselves from the responsibility of providing work life initiatives for modern day employees.

Work Life Balance is not just a zero sum game:

The urgent need of the hour from the perspective of modern organizations is not just try to focus on achieving balance between work and life by treating them as separate, interconnected, and mutually beneficial domains, but rather look at work and life as an integrated, composite system that includes work, home, community and self. It should not be seen as just a "zero sum game", where you take something from one basket and put into another, but should be seen as an integral composite framework where the aim is to achieve overall satisfaction and happiness. Work and Life domains are an integral part of each other that cannot be seen as separate entities. Satisfaction in one cannot be achieved at the cost of the other.

The rising need for Work Life Balance Initiatives:

Clearly the modern day organizations have realized the importance of implementing work life initiative programs in their organizational fold. The following is a brief list of factors that have contributed to the emerging need of achieving the much needed work life balance for employees in the organizations:

— **Demographic changes:** there have been significant demographic changes in the structural fold of the workforce, by and large in many nations the average age of working populations has considerably increased, there has been change in structural composition of families from joint families to nuclear families even in Asian and middle eastern countries, the number of employees having elder care responsibilities has also increased.

- **Composition of Labour Force:** There has been a rapid transformation in the composition of labour force; women now have become a major integral part of labour force even from the perspective of Arab countries. The increasing feminization of labour force brings its new challenges for instituting of work life initiatives, as employers need to care for special needs of women.

- **Decline of the role of welfare state:** In many countries across the globe the model of welfare states has declined substantially, with the state rolling back its frontiers, framework of care has rapidly changed. All this has resulted in greater commodification of parameters of care. This has increased substantially work life conflict as employees have been burdened with extra care responsibilities, which makes the need for achieving the illusive balance between work and life demands all the more warranted.

- **Changes in legislative frameworks & social expectations:** There have been wide scale changes in legal frameworks that warrant companies to limit their maximum hours, provide leave for maternity, paternity or elderly care. Moreover the societal expectations from the companies have also significantly changed as people expect companies to be more responsive and caring towards their employees and discharge their ever increasing corporate social responsibility obligations to the best of their abilities. Organizations are also intent in projecting themselves as "employers of choice" in the increasingly complex and competitive modern environments for attracting and retaining the best possible talent in their work force. In such changing business and social landscapes, work life balance programs have become a part of modern companies' social, moral and ethical agenda for improving employee satisfaction as well as overall firm productivity and performance.

— **Changes in the nature of work:** The nature of work has also changed significantly; there has been a substantial increase of competition and work intensification which has created high levels of stress for employees. There has been an increase of roles and expectations of employees in their work domain as well as in their family or life domain (Bond et.al, 2002). For placating the stressful environments that workers are exposed to, companies have started initiating better work life balance initiatives to lessen work life conflicts.

— **Emergence of Corporate Social Responsibility:** The new agenda of companies is not just to solely focus on their narrow bottom line of improving profits but focus on their triple bottom line that is their financial, societal and environmental obligations. In the context of the expanded new avatar of corporate social responsibilities and obligations, work life balance initiatives hold their own special place of relevance and importance. One cannot forget that modern days companies are responsible to all their stakeholders; investors, managers, employees and society at large.

From the aforementioned reasons, it can be gauged that work life initiatives have become a much required necessity for modern day firms. These initiatives can bring about improved performance and reputation for the company as well as enhance substantially levels of employee satisfaction, motivation and commitment.

HR needs to play a key role in Work Life Balance Initiatives:

Work life balance initiatives have assumed a new stage of importance for modern organizations. HR has to play a key role in launching and institutionalization of these work life initiative programs. Following is a brief list of reasons that necessitate the strategic involvement of HR:

- New focus of modern organizations is to achieve success in their triple bottom line, HR as a strategic business partner has to involve itself in processes that lead to improvements in overall performance, productivity and reputation for modern firms.
- HR professionals are very much the employee champions; HR has to ensure that employees face least work life conflicts so that their efficiency is not sacrificed, and their potential can be fully tapped into.
- HR professionals are specialists in dealing with personnel issues and problems; work life conflict is a major arena that can generate high level of stress and discomfort for employees.
- HR professionals help to form the crucial bridge for connecting employees with the organization, no department is better placed or more familiar with individual employee needs and requirements than HR department.
- HR professionals also play a key role in job designing; therefore their involvement in designing work place initiatives is warranted as they are familiar with the increasing physical, mental and emotional stresses that employees face in new job environments. Moreover HR helps develop competencies through its regular involvement in developing and imparting employee training.
- HR department in organizations often handle compliance and legal issues, many work life provisions have become mandatory by law.

Myriad Benefits associated with Work Life Balance Initiatives:

It has become evident that gone are the days when companies could treat domains of work and life as totally unconnected and separate. Mandated by law, pressurized by societal expectations and driven by the increasing burden of moral and ethical obligations, modern day companies have become more receptive to the needs of instituting work life balance programs. Companies have begun to realize that their involvement in work life balance programs should be seen as an investment as such initiative can and do provide myriad benefits for virtually all the stakeholders of the organization.

— **Increased Profitability**—Work life initiatives can enhance overall profitability of the company. In a study of 130 announcements in the Wall Street Journal of work life initiatives instituted by modern companies, it was found that such announcements create significant increases in share price index of instituting firms (Arthur, 2003). Moreover work life initiatives help the firm achieve better its obligations in relation to its triple bottom line (financial, environment and social).

— **Higher Productivity**—Work life balance programs can also help either directly or indirectly in improving organizational performance and productivity. It can be conjectured that better work life initiatives can improve job satisfaction of employees, and greater levels of job satisfaction can ultimately translate into superior organizational performance and productivity.

— **Increased OCB**—Work life balance programs can also facilitate greater levels of organizational citizenship behavior (OCB) in employees such as altruism, courtesy, conscientiousness, civic virtue and sportsmanship. These extra role behaviors exhibited by employees can prove crucial in improving overall organizational performance (Lambert, 2000).

— **Employee Turnover & Morale**: Better work life balance programs can help in improving levels of employee morale and loyalty as workers feel valued by their organizations. Moreover these programs can help reduce employee turnover and absenteeism in employees and thereby prove cost effective for the organizations.

— **Recruitment & Retention**—It has been found that the companies that do create work life balance programs often rise up many notches in the eyes of employees as "employers of choice". Being an employer of choice proves beneficial for the company not only in recruiting more talented employees but also in significantly improving its corporate brand image in the eyes of consumers "as a caring and responsible" organization. Higher reputation and image even may improve willingness of workers to work in the organization even at lower salaries in light of the benefits offered by the organization in terms of balancing their work life demands.

Simple Steps for implementing Work Life Balance Programs:

There is no denying that work life balance programs are here to stay. Companies therefore need to create a practical framework for the implementation and institutionalization of these programs in light of their unique competencies, needs and capacities. Some of the generic steps that can prove useful in this regard are listed below:

• **Tune in the Organisational Vision:** For work life balance programs to be successful, it is necessary that the commitment to these programs be adequately reflected in the overall organisational vision and mission of the company. Employees are deemed to be the most important assets for any company, therefore programs that facilitate a better synchronisation of their work and non work demands should be given top priority. The commitment to work life balance should be a part and parcel of the strategic intent of the company and not just used as a cosmetic tool for catering to legal stipulations and standards.

- **Perform Organisational Diagnostics**—It is essential for the company to carry out well planned organisational diagnostics to identify the specific needs and requirements of the firm for instituting work life balance programs. Every company would have its own unique needs and requirements given the unique composition of its work force, the nature of work it deals in, and the kind of local or regional business landscape that it operates in. Organisational diagnostics can help uncover the need for such programs as well as chalk out a tentative road map for outlining how these needs and expectations can be fulfilled.
- **Allow HR to Take the Lead:** In performance of organisational diagnostics and other processes of implementation and compliance, allow the HR department to assume natural leadership. HR professionals are employee champions and personnel specialists, therefore they would be in a better position to assess, analyse and plan for the divergent needs of the employees. Moreover work life demands are individual worker specific, and HR professionals are competent in resolving issues with individual employees.
- **Encourage Employee Participation:** Try to keep channels of communication open for designing work life balance programs. As these programs are being created for helping employees, they must be allowed to participate fully in the process, provide their suggestions, and help in identification of their unique needs and expectations. A top down approach

in implementing work life balance programs would rarely achieve its intended objectives. Actively seek employee suggestions using questionnaires and interviews to see how effectively employee needs are being catered to. Furthermore employee participation is also warranted for assessing the outcomes of the instituted programs.

- **Analyze the available options:** A careful well balanced analysis must be made of the different options available for work life balance programs. Some of these options are already mandated by law, other options need to be properly analyzed in relation to the specific needs and requirements of employees. Some common ways of instituting work life balance initiatives are shown below :

1. Flex the Time : create alternative work schedules, compressed work week, allow for voluntary part time work, reduce hours in view of employee needs, allow employees to take in phased retirement in view of their commitments.
2. Flex the place: Resort to telecommuting—allow the workers to work from home. However this would depend on the nature of the job and responsibilities associated with the job.
3. Flex the Job: Try to redesign the job so that employees can save time without sacrificing efficiency, allow job sharing for specific employee requests or in special circumstances.
4. Flex the Benefits: Allow employees to take temporary leave in emergency or special situations, provide them with leaves for dependant care, and have provision of employee assistance and wellness programs in place. Try to abide by legal stipulations for preventing being embroiled in costly legal battles.

- **Constant Review & Feedback**: Work life balance programs need to be constantly monitored and reviewed by the organisation to see whether they are fulfilling the intended objectives. Given the inherent dynamism associated with these programs, the company must carefully review the impact of these programs from time to time. Furthermore through collection of regular feedback from employees ascertain what further improvements can be or need to be incorporated in these programs.

Some common problems associated with work life initiatives:

While work life balance has been acknowledged as an important factor in creating greater motivation, satisfaction and involvement of work force, nevertheless there are some significant challenges which the modern firms face in implementing these frameworks:

1. Time is finite: One of key challenge is determination of how the allocation of time needs to be decided between work and non work demands, since time is a finite quantity. Finite time gives you only a limited leverage for being flexible in relation to employee demands.
2. One size cannot fit all: Work life balance programs are relatively specific to the type of the organisation and the nature of the work that the employees are engaged in. It is not possible for delineating a generic carte blanche list of work life balance initiatives for all organisations as each has different needs and different requirements. The mindset of one size fits all approach is not practical or feasible in the context of developing work life balance programs (Hyman & Summers, 2004).
3. Limited Employee Power and Voice: Another major stumbling block in implementation of these programs

is the highly limited employee power and voice which is provided in modern organizations. With loss of the power of employee unions internationally, the asymmetrical relationship between employers and employees seems to have been greatly exacerbated (Cully et. al, 1999). Limited employee voice and the skewed power distribution in favour of management leads to implementation of work life initiatives in a highly selective top down format that prevents the holistic involvement and participation of employees.

4. Intense Competition and Business Pressure: Companies on their side seem to be sandwiched between intense competition to perform and business pressures of increasing their profits. In such an environment where harsh economic conditions scuttle the productivity of firms, it is difficult for firms to draw the fine line of balancing work life demands for employees. As a result in many cases employers institute these programs only as temporary adjustments which serve as mere cosmetic entities rather than functional frameworks.

5. No yard stick for standardization: A common stumbling block for companies is that there are no set standards for creating formalization and standardization of these programs. With needs of the company showing high degree of divergence, management is often handicapped by absence of a practical road map that can guide the entire process.

6. Low levels of Employee Participation: Ironically it has been found that employees in many cases are reluctant to avail of these work life balance programs on their own as they feel it would be a reflection of their help seeking behaviour. Help seeking attitude is often frowned upon in corporate circles as being a sign of weakness. By seeking assistance employees do not want to project themselves as shirking away from the job or challenges associated with jobs (Viega et. al, 2004).

7. A Big organisation thing: Work life balance programs are still very much practiced only by large public and private sector organisations. Smaller firms provide very little of employee assistance in the form of work life balance initiatives. These programs are most likely to be provided by public sector or large private sector corporations that have strong unions or high ratio of female representation in their labour force (Cully, et.al. 1999).

In summation it can be stated that though there are many challenges, companies need to adopt an aggressive and proactive approach in instituting work life balance programs. The action of companies in institution of these programs should not be seen as a mere submission to legal stipulations but should be seen as a reflection of their genuine eagerness to create greater employee satisfaction. The focus should be levied not in bifurcating equal amounts of time for work and non work demands, but in creating a flexible and understanding environment that is sensitive to the needs of modern day workers. One cannot forget that employees are the most important assets for any company and hence their satisfaction and well being should be of utmost importance for all companies.

Useful Takeaways from Chapter

- Work and life demands should be seen as an integrated composite entity.
- In the industrial era it was erroneously believed that work and life could be seen as two separate unconnected domains.
- "Work life" balance can be seen as the reconciliation between paid work and life.
- Work life balance programs can help improve employee motivation, help firms gain competitive advantage and emerge as employers of choice.
- Demographic changes, feminization of labour force, declining framework of care, changes in legislative frameworks and societal expectations have all created the need for work life balance initiatives.
- Work life balance programs are part of the overarching corporate social responsibility agenda.
- HR has to play a leading role in planning, implementing and institutionalization of work life balance programs.
- In spite of challenges, work life balance programs must be initiated in companies through active employee participation and effective organizational diagnostics.

BIBLIOGRAPHY

Allen, R. (1985) : Four Phases for Bringing About Cultural Change, in Gaining Control of the Corporate Culture, eds R. Kilmann, M. Saxton, R. Serpa, Jossey Bass, San Francisco.

Arthur, M. M. (2003). Share price reactions to work-family initiatives: An institutional perspective. Academy of Management Journal, 46 (4): 497-505.

Baker, G. P.; Jensen, Michael C.; Murphy, Kevin J. (1988) Compensation And Incentives: Practice Vs. Theory. The Journal of Finance; 43: (3) 593-616.

Bamford, D. R. and Forrester, P. L. (2003) 'Managing planned and emergent change within an operations management environment', International Journal of Operations & Production Management, 23(5), pp. 546-564.

Barber, A. E. 1998. *Recruiting employees*. Thousand Oaks, CA: Sage Publications.

Barger, N.J and Kirby, L.K. (1995). The challenge of change in organisations. Helping employees thrive in the new frontier. USA: Davies-Black.

Baron, J.; & Kreps, D. (1999): Strategic Human Resources: Frameworks for General Managers. New York, NY: John Wiley.

Bloom N. et al. (2005) Management practices: the impact on company performance. Centre Piece, 10 (2) 2-6

Bond, S., Hyman, J., Summers, J. and Wise, S. (2002), Family-Friendly Working? Putting Policy into Practice, York Publishing Services, York.

Boxall, P, and Purcell, J. (2003) Strategy and human resource management. Palgrave Macmillan,

Breaugh, J. A.; & Starke, M. (2000): Research on employee recruitment: So many studies, so many remaining questions. Journal of Management, 26 (3): 405-434.

Campion, M.A., Mumford, T.V., Morgeson, F.P., & Nahrgang, J.D. (2005). Work redesign: Eight obstacles and opportunities. Human Resource Management, Vol 44, No. 4 pp.367-390

Cully, M., Woodland, S., O'Reilly, A. and Dix, G. (1999), Britain at Work, Routledge, London.

Delery, J. E.; & Shaw, J. D. (2001): The strategic management of people in work organizations: Review, synthesis, and extension. Research in Personnel and Human Resources Management, Vol. 20: 165-197. Greenwich, CT: Elsevier.

DeNisi, A. S.; & Kluger, A. N. (2000): Feedback effectiveness: Can 360-degree appraisals be improved? Academy of Management Executive, 14 (1): 129-139.

Dex, S. and Smith, C. (2002), The Nature and Pattern of Family-Friendly Employment Policies in Britain, The Policy Press, Bristol.

Fernie, S.; & Metcalf, D. (1999): It's not what you pay it's the way that you pay it and that's what gets results: Jockeys' pay and performance. Labour: Review of labour economics and industrial relations, 13 (2): 385-411.

Fisher C.D. & Thomas, J.(1982) The other face of performance appraisal. Human Resources Management, 21, pp. 24-26.

Fletcher, C. (2001): Performance appraisal and management: The developing research agenda. Journal of Occupational and Organizational Psychology, 74: 473-487.

Ghorpade, J. (2000): Managing five paradoxes of 360-degree feedback. Academy of Management Executive, 14 (1): 140-150.

Godard, J. (2004) A critical assessment of the high performance paradigm. British Journal of Industrial Relations, 42: (2) 349-378.

Goleman, D. (1995). Emotional Intelligence. New York: Bantam Books.

Goleman, D. (1998). Working with emotional intelligence. New York: Bantam Books

Goleman, D., Boyatzis, R.E., & McKee, A. (2002). Primal Leadership: Realising the Power of Emotional Intelligence. Boston, MA: Harvard Business School Press

Grugulis I. (2007), Skills, Training and Human Resources Management: *A Critical text*. Basingstoke: Palgrave Macmillan.

Hackman, J.R. and Oldham, G.R. (1976) <u>Motivation through the design of work; Test of a theory.</u> Organizational Behaviour and Human Performance. 16; 250-279

Heyes, J. Stuart, M. (1996), 'Does training matter? Employee experiences and attitudes' *Human Resources Management Journal*, Vol. 6, No. 3,pp. 7-21.

Hyman, J., & Summers, J. (2004). Lacking balance? Work-life employment practices in the modern economy. Personnel Review, 33 (4): 418-429.

Kanter, R. M., Stein, B. A. and Jick, T. D. (1992) The Challenge of Organizational Change (New York: The Free Press).

Kaplan, R. S. and D. P. Norton, (1992), "The Balanced Scorecard—Measures that drive performance", *Harvard Business Review* Jan-Feb, pp. 71-79

Kay, J.(1993) *The Foundations of corporate success.* Oxford University Press, Oxford.

Keep E. (1989), Corporate Training Strategies: the vital component? In J. Storey (ed.), *New Perspective on Human Resources Management*, London: Rout ledge.

Kolb. D A. (1986) *The User's Guide for the Learning-Style Inventory: A Manual for Teachers and Trainers.* McBer & Company. Boston, MA

Kotter, J. P. (1996) Leading Change (Boston, MA: Harvard Business School Press).

Lambert, S.J. (2000). Added benefits: The link between work-life benefits and organisational citizenship behavior. Academy of Management Journal, 43 (5): 801-815.

Locke, E. A. & Latham, G.P. (2002) Building a practically useful theory of goal setting and task motivation: a 35-year odyssey. American Psychologist, 57:(9):705-717.

Marchington, M.; & Wilkinson, A. (2005) Human Resource Management at Work: People Management and Development. 3rd ed., London: CIPD.

Mayer, J. and Salovey, P. (1997) `What is emotional intelligence?", in Salovey, P. and Sluyter, D. (Eds), Emotional Development and Emotional Intelligence: Implications for Educators, Basic Books, New York, NY

Parker, S.K., Wall, T.D., Cordery, J.L. (2001). Future work design research and practice: Towards an elaborated model of work design. Journal of Occupational and Organizational Psychology, 74: 413-440

Parker, S. and Wall, T. (1998) 'A critique of existing theory and research' (chapter 3) Job and Work Design. Sage

Peters, T, J, and Waterman, R, H, J r (1982), *In Search of Excellence*. New York: Harper & Row.

Pfeffer, J. (1995): Producing sustainable competitive advantage through the effective management of people. Academy of Management Executive, 9 (1): 55-72.

Roe, R. A. (1999): Work performance: A multiple regulation perspective. In C. L. Cooper & I. T. Robertson (eds.): International Review of Industrial and Organisational Psychology: 14: 231-335. Chichester: Wiley.

Rousseau, D. M. (2001): Schema, promise and mutuality: The building blocks of the psychological contract. Journal of Occupational and Organizational Psychology. 74 (4) 511-42.

Salgado, Jesus F. (1999): Personnel selection methods. In: C. L. Cooper & I. T. Robertson (eds.): International Review of Industrial and Organizational Psychology, 14: 1-54. Chichester: Wiley.

Schein, E. (1985). Organisational Psychology, 3rd ed., Prentice Hall, Englewood Cliffs, NJ

Storey, J, (Ed,) (2001), *Human Resource Management: A Critical Text,* 2nd edition, London: Thomson Learning

Veiga, J. F., Baldridge, D. C., & Eddleston, K. A. (2004). Toward understanding employee reluctance to participate in family-friendly programs.

Wall, T. D.; & Martin, R. (1994): Job and work design. In C. L. Cooper & I. T. Robertson (eds.): Key Reviews in Managerial Psychology: 158-188. Chichester: Wiley.

Watson, T (2004) 'HRM and critical social science analysis' Journal of Management Studies 41 (2) 447-468.

Weick, K.E. Quinn, R.E. (1999) Organizational Change and Development, *Annual Review of Psychology*, Vol.50, No. 1. (1999), pp. 361-386.